# John Newton: Letters of a Slave Trader

# John Newton: Letters of a Slave Trader

## paraphrased by
# Dick Bohrer

**MOODY PRESS**

CHICAGO

© 1983 by
THE MOODY BIBLE INSTITUTE
OF CHICAGO

These letters were originally written to the Reverend T. Haweis, D.D., and were first published in 1764. This paraphrase is based upon *Out of the Depths:* Autobiography of the Rev. John Newton (Chicago: Moody, n.d.).

ISBN:0-8024-0158-9

**Library of Congress Cataloging in Publication Data**

Bohrer, Dick.
   John Newton, letters of a slave trader.

   Adaptation of: An authentic narrative of some remarkable and interesting particulars in the life of John Newton originally published 1764.
   1. Newton, John, 1725-1807. 2. Church of England—England—Clergy—Biography. I. Newton, John, 1725-1807. An authentic narrative of some remarkable and interesting particulars in the life of John Newton.
II. Title. III. Title: Letters of a slave trader.
BX5199.N55B64   1983      283′.3      82-22894
ISBN 0-8024-0158-9

   1 2 3 4 5 6 7 Printing/LC/Year 87 86 85 84 83

*Printed in the United States of America*

# Contents

# Prologue

John Newton (1725-1807) was born the son of a British merchant sea captain. His mother died just before his seventh birthday, while his father was at sea.

After a disturbing and unsettled childhood—with countless disciplinary problems—Newton joined the Royal Navy. He was arrested for attempting to escape from ship. In Africa, he was held in captivity by his employer's black wife, who treated him as a slave. He later became involved in the slave trade himself. When about twenty-three years of age, during a violent storm at sea, he finally turned over his life to God.

Despite his newfound faith, Newton continued in the slave traffic until 1755, when he determined to pursue the ministry. In 1764, he became curate of Olney in Buckinghamshire. In 1779, he was appointed vicar of Saint Mary, Woolnoth, in London. During his ministry, Newton wrote several hymns —some of which are still popular, including "How

Sweet the Name of Jesus Sounds" and "Glorious Things of Thee Are Spoken."

John Newton would never lose his sense of wonder at the grace of God extended to him, "an infidel and libertine, a servant of slaves." That wonder he expressed in perhaps his best-known hymn, "Amazing Grace":

Amazing grace! how sweet the sound
That saved a wretch like me!
I once was lost, but now am found,
Was blind, but now I see.

'Twas grace that taught my heart to fear,
And grace my fears relieved;
How precious did that grace appear
The hour I first believed!

Through many dangers, toils and snares,
I have already come;
'Tis grace hath brought me safe thus far,
And grace will lead me home.

When we've been there ten thousand years,
Bright shining as the sun,
We've no less days to sing God's praise
Than when we first begun.

1779

# Letter 1

## Reasons for Writing the Account

My dear Haweis:

I want you to read between the lines of this first letter to you. I'm going to tell you the story of God's great dealings in my life. But before I get to the specifics, I want to give you an overview.

I'm sure you've meditated on God's promise to the Israelites in Deuteronomy 8:2. Remember, they were struggling with difficulties in the wilderness —difficulties that were aggravated by their own perversity and distrust of God. No matter how kind He was to them, they couldn't comprehend the reasons for their distresses. They couldn't see that God had some kind of good intention.

Then Moses told them that a future happy time was drawing near when they would come to the land God had promised them. There they would be at home and have rest from all their fears and troubles. Then they would look back with pleasure on what they were now finding so hard to bear.

He told them, "Thou shalt remember all the way which the LORD thy God led thee ... in the wilderness" (Deuteronomy 8:2).

These words give real comfort to us if we apply them spiritually. They're addressed to all who are passing through the wilderness of this world to a heavenly Canaan. Everyone who is seeking eternal rest in the unshakable Kingdom will be more than conqueror over the trials of life if he keeps his eye fixed on the Lord. Even if we feel all the weaknesses of our fallen nature and in ignorance and unbelief mistake His dealings with us, we would rejoice if we knew all He knows.

Once we can look back and see all the way the Lord has led us, we'll see that mercy and goodness directed every step. We'll see that what we once called adversities and evils were really blessings we could not have done well without. Nothing befalls us without a cause. No trouble comes on us sooner or presses on us more heavily or more continually than we need.

God uses our many afflictions to bring us into the good of all He has done for us. Our reward will be that "exceeding and eternal weight of glory" that the Lord has prepared for them that love Him (2 Corinthians 4:17).

When we look back and see what the Lord has brought us through over the years, we can see how He has woven this thread with that one, wonderfully connecting one event with another. Our greatest advantages may have seemed hardly worth our notice when they happened. Sometimes we've escaped great dangers, not by any wisdom or foresight of our own, but only by the intervention of some circumstance quite beyond what we would have desired or thought.

God does overrule His people and guard them through all their wanderings and lead them in a way they know not.

I believe, dear friend, that we'll all be able to acknowledge that this is true—some more than others. Though the outward circumstances of some people have varied little from those about them, often an inward change in a secret way—unnoticed by others and barely noticed by themselves—will indicate that God is gradually drawing them to Himself. Though they now have a happy assurance that they know Him and love Him and have passed from death to life, yet they can't pin down the precise time and manner.

Some He selects so that He can showcase the depth and richness of His grace and power. He lets their natural rebellion and wickedness have full scope. He cuts others short; but some He spares, even though they are wild sinners. When their reputation is so vile that everyone expects they'll get their just desert, God plucks them as brands out of the fire to make them monuments of His mercy and a real encouragement to others. In a moment, it seems, they are convinced, pardoned, and changed.

That is as fantastic as the creation of the world.

It is entirely the Lord's doing, and it is marvelous in the eyes of anyone who is not already blinded by prejudice and unbelief.

Saul of Tarsus hated Jesus of Nazareth and persecuted His disciples relentlessly. He'd been a terror to the church in Jerusalem and was going to Damascus to threaten and slaughter the ones there who loved the Lord. He thought he was doing God a service by destroying a whole sect. It didn't bother him that he was terrifying his own countrymen.

And then the Lord Jesus, whom he hated and opposed, checked him right at the height of his rage. He called this bitter persecutor to the honor of an apostle and inspired him to preach with zeal and earnestness the faith he had so recently tried to destroy.

Every age seems to have people like that—people who have made a habit of evil, who have had to look up to see bottom. In the day of God's power they are saved and transformed. They become examples to other believers, giving them an opportunity to praise God for His remarkable grace.

I was one of those. To whom much has been forgiven, the same loves much (see Luke 7:47). The apostle Paul could say, "His grace which was bestowed upon me was not in vain; but I labored more abundantly than they all"(1 Corinthians 15:10). Others, loving much, have labored much, becoming a burning and shining light. The manner of their conversion was hardly more unique than the whole course of their lives from then on until they died.

It has not been that way with me. I am ashamed of myself, for I have given God a very bad return on His investment. If the question were only one of tracing God's patience and longsuffering or examining the wonderful way He inserted His favor into the life of so unworthy a sinner as myself, then I know of no case more extraordinary than mine. He softened the hardest heart when the power of His grace softened mine. He mercifully pardoned enormous transgressions when He pardoned mine.

A number of people have urged me to preserve my story, but I find it difficult to tell *my* story. I don't want to talk or write about *myself*. And then, too, people who like to pour over the dirt in another's life make a lot out of such stories as mine.

The psalmist tells me that a certain reserve in this kind of thing is proper: "Come and hear, all ye that fear God, and I will declare what He hath done for my soul" (Psalm 66:16). And our Lord cautions us against casting our pearls before swine. The pearls of a Christian are, perhaps, his choice experiences of the Lord's power and love in the things that concern his own soul. Such things shouldn't be made public, lest we give the unsaved something to make light of that they do not understand.

I sent one friend whom I respected eight letters. But they have fallen into the wrong hands.

Since you and other friends of mine have asked me to rewrite them to bring my Lord praise and to establish the faith of His people, well—I am willing. If God will be glorified by this, and if His children will be comforted or instructed by what I have to tell them of His goodness, then I will be satisfied.

I will have to rely on my memory as I failed to make copies of those letters. I hope you will excuse me if I do not restrict myself to narrative, but comment now and then on what I am writing. That way I will be able to write freely and frankly.

# Letter 2
## My Youth

My dear Haweis:

My mother died when I was just under seven. I was born July 24, 1725, and she died July 11, 1732. Her death was one of the great turning points of my life.

She had hoped I would eventually enter the ministry, so she captured every moment to educate me properly. She was a godly, experienced Christian, a Dissenter, and I was her only child. She was not well, and she was rather shy, but she was tireless in teaching me. I was not more than three when she taught me to speak fluently. When I was four, I could easily read any common book. She stored my memory with many Scripture portions and chapters, catechisms, hymns, and poems.

I was as willing to learn as she was to teach. Somehow, I wasn't interested in noisy games with other children. When I was six, I began to learn Latin. But before I had time to know much of it, the Lord took my mother Home.

Although in later years I sinned away the advantages of those early lessons, they acted as a real restraint upon me. They returned again and again, and it was a long time before I could wholly shake them off. When the Lord finally brought me to Himself, I profited immensely, because the Word of God had already been engrafted on my heart.

My father was at sea when Mother died. A commander in the Mediterranean trade, he came home the following year and soon married again. My new mother didn't pay any attention to my lessons but let me play with and learn the ways of careless and profane children. She sent me away to a boarding school where the teacher almost broke my spirit and my love for learning. I stayed two years; but near the end of that time a new teacher came who noticed how much I really loved learning. I took to Latin again like a mother tongue. Before I was ten, I was reading Tully and Virgil. But he pushed me too fast. Years later, when I turned to Latin again, I found all I had learned had vanished.

When I was eleven, my father took me to sea with him. A man of remarkable good sense and great knowledge of the world, he took great care of my morals. But he could never be a mother to me. He had been raised in Spain and taught to keep distance and severity in his manner. I was always afraid of him and overawed. In no way did I want to be like him, so he didn't have much influence on me.

When I was twelve, I was thrown from a horse and narrowly missed being impaled on the sharp trunks of a hedgerow newly cut down. I couldn't help but notice that my escape from death was miraculous, and my conscience needled me to consider where I would have gone had I been killed. For a time after that, I behaved myself, but soon I indulged my secret sins again. I often repeated these struggles between sin and conscience, and every relapse sank me into still greater depths of wickedness.

A few months into my fifteenth year, I had the chance of a lifetime to take a position at Alicant, Spain. But I was so erratic in behavior and unruly that the job went to another person. Religion at this time had no effect on me, but I eagerly absorbed every evil influence. Occasionally, since I was fond of reading, a good book would come my way. One, Benet's *Christian Oratory*, presented a style of life that appealed to me. I began to pray, read the Scripture, and keep a diary. But none of this was built on any solid foundation, and I soon drifted on to new things. I became worse than before. Instead of praying, I learned to curse and blaspheme.

I was once roused from my wickedness by the loss of a very close friend. We had agreed to sneak on board a man-of-war on a Sunday, but I got to our rendezvous point too late. He and other friends had gone on without me, and the rowboat had overturned. My friend and several others were drowned. The fact that my life had been preserved profoundly moved me at the time, but this too was soon forgotten. I think I took up and laid aside a religious profession three or four different times before I was sixteen, but my heart was insincere.

I saw the necessity of religion as a means of escaping hell, but I loved sin and was unwilling to forsake it. I was so perverse that, when I determined to do things I knew were sinful and contrary to my duty, I would stop first and have devotions. I begrudged every minute of the delay, but curbed myself until I was finished. Once done, I would rush into my foolish plan.

My last reform was the most remarkable one. I lived the life of a Pharisee, doing everything that might be expected from a religious person entirely ignorant of God's righteousness, but desirous of establishing his own. I spent the greater part of each day reading the Bible, meditating, and praying. I often fasted and even abstained from eating animal products for three months. I would hardly answer a question for fear of speaking an idle word. I mourned my former conduct—often with tears.

I became an ascetic and renounced society to avoid temptation. I continued this for more than two years without much interruption. It was poor religion. It left me, in many respects, under the power of sin. It tended to make me gloomy, stupid, unsociable, and useless.

Such was my frame of mind when a book called *Characteristics*, by Lord Shaftesbury (1671-1713), came to my attention. Actually, the title allured me, and the style and manner of his prose really appealed to me. The second essay in the book, entitled "A Rhapsody," completely intrigued me. Nothing could be more suited to my romantic mind than this pompous declamation. I swallowed his philosophy eagerly, giving no thought at all to where it might lead me. I thought the author a most religious person. I was only too happy to follow him. The book was always in my hand. I read it so often I could nearly repeat the "Rhapsody" verbatim. No immediate effect followed; but it operated in me like a slow poison and prepared the way for all that came after.

In December 1742, I returned home from a voyage. I thought I would go to sea again, but Father had other plans. I had no interest in business, and I knew little of the ways of the world. I was a visionary, fond of the contemplative life—a medley of religion, philosophy, and laziness. The last thing I wanted to do was to rise at five and go to work!

Finally, a friend of Father's, a merchant in Liverpool, suggested that he send me to Jamaica, where he would see to it that I prospered. I agreed to this and was on the point of setting out the following week when Father sent me on business a few miles beyond Maidstone, in Kent.

This little journey, which was to have been only for three or four days, sparked a sudden, remarkable turn in my life that roused me completely from my laziness.

"The way of man is not in himself: it is not in man that walketh to direct his steps" (Jeremiah 10:23).

# Letter 3

## My Early Life as a Sailor

My dear Haweis:

The folks I went to visit were intimate friends of my mother's. Because their interest in our family had cooled after Father's second marriage, I had heard nothing of them for many years.

Actually, I was not all that interested in going to see them, and I almost passed by without going in. But I did go in. I was recognized at first sight and shown the kindest reception as the child of a dear, deceased friend.

These folks had two daughters. The eldest, as I learned some years later, had been considered by her mother and mine as a future wife for me from the time of her birth. I would not say that what Mother predicted was ever going to happen, but I

13

felt there was something remarkable about it all when I learned of it. Any kind of arrangement between the two families had, of course, broken off long before. And now I was going off to a foreign country and had only called to say good-bye.

But almost from my very first sight of this girl (she was then under fourteen), I felt an affection for her that never faded or lost its influence for a single moment in my heart. In its intensity, it equaled all that the writers of romance have imagined. I knew it would endure forever.

Even though soon after this I lost all sense of religion and became deaf to any of the cautions of my conscience, none of the misery I experienced ever banished her a single hour from my waking thoughts for seven years following. Hardly anything less than this violent and commanding passion would have been sufficient to waken me from the gloominess I had sunk into. And later, when I made shipwreck of my faith, hope, and conscience, my love for this person was the only remaining principle that in any degree took their place. The bare possibility that I might see her again was the only thing restraining me from crimes against myself and others.

Courtship normally is a time for pleasantries —mutual affection, the consent of friends, and a date to look forward to—especially when it is governed by the will and fear of God. But I did not dare mention this to her friends or to my own, nor for a long time to her. I could not make any proposals or give any indication to anyone, because a dark fire was locked up in my breast, a fire that uniquely gave me a constant uneasiness and greatly weakened my sense of religion. In fact, it opened the way for all sorts of foolishness in my private life. Though my love for her seemed to be an incentive for me to do great things to make her proud of me, in reality—when you come right down to the bottom line—it didn't make me a better man. Oh, I had great resolves, but they didn't produce a thing.

But I did realize that it would be absolutely impossible for me to live as far away as Jamaica for four or five years. So I decided I would not go. I was afraid to tell my father the real reason, and I was afraid to lie to him. So, without giving him any notice, I stayed three weeks in Kent—instead of three days. I figured that by the time I got back to London the ship would have sailed, and the opportunity I had been planning would have evaporated.

I was right. When I returned to London, I learned that my father was, indeed, angry at my disobedience, but not as angry as I had imagined.

A short time later, I sailed with a friend of my father's to Venice. The common sailors on board were certainly not the finest examples of decency and order, but they were fun to be with. I began to relax from the sober self-discipline I had cultivated for the last two years. Though I made a few faint efforts to stop, I never recovered from this decline as I had from the ones that preceded it—I was now making large strides toward total apostasy from God.

The most remarkable warning I received (and

the last one) was a dream that made a very strong, though not a lasting, impression on my mind.

The scene was the harbor of Venice where we had just been. I thought it was night and that it was my turn to stand watch on the dock. As I was walking to and fro by myself, a man brought me a ring with the express order to keep it carefully. He assured me that, while I preserved that ring, I would be happy and successful. But if I lost it or parted with it, I could expect nothing but trouble and misery.

I accepted the present and the terms willingly, knowing that I would indeed care for it and gloating that now I would have my happiness in my own keeping.

Then a second person came to me and, seeing the ring on my finger, asked some questions about it. I readily told him its value, and he said he was astonished that I was so gullible in expecting such effects from a mere ring. He argued with me for some time and then urged me to throw the ring away.

At first I was shocked at such a suggestion, but he kept telling me how foolish I was. Then I began to consider his reasons and to doubt the original story. At last, I pulled it from my finger and dropped it over the ship's side into the water.

At the same instant, a terrible fire burst out from a range of mountains, some distance behind the city of Venice. I saw the hills as distinctly as if I were awake, and they were all in flames.

Too late, I realized how foolish I had been. My tempter, with an insulting sneer, informed me that all the mercy of God reserved for me was lodged in the ring I had willfully thrown away. He said I would have to go with him to the burning mountains and that all the flames I saw had been kindled on my account. I trembled in great agony. But the dream continued.

As I stood there, hopelessly condemning myself, a third person—or the same one who brought the ring the first time (I'm not certain which)—came to me, demanding to know why I was grieving. I told him plainly, confessing that I had ruined myself willfully and deserved no pity.

He blamed my foolishness and asked if I would be any wiser the next time, if I had my ring back again. I could hardly answer; I thought it was gone for good. Before I even had time to answer, this unexpected friend plunged into the water just at the spot where I had dropped the ring. He returned in a moment, bringing it with him.

The moment he came on board, the flames in the mountains were extinguished, and my evil seducer left me. With joy and gratitude, I went up to my kind deliverer with my hand opened to receive my ring again. But he refused to return it.

He said, "If you were to be entrusted with this ring again, you would soon bring yourself into the same distress. You are not able to keep it, so I will preserve it for you. Whenever you need it, I will produce it in your behalf."

I awoke astonished. I could hardly eat, sleep, or work for two or three days.

But the impression soon wore off, and I totally

forgot it. It hardly returned to my mind until several years later.

A time was coming soon, though I didn't know it then, when I would find myself in circumstances very nearly resembling the ones suggested by this dream. Had my mind been open, I would have recognized my grand enemy seducing me to willfully renounce my religious professions and involve myself in his complicated crimes. I would have seen that he was delighted with my agonies, waiting only for permission to seize and bear my soul away to his place of torment.

I would also have seen Jesus, whom I had persecuted and defied, rebuking the adversary and claiming me for His own. He would have plucked me as a brand from the fire and declared to Satan, "Deliver him from going down to the pit: I have found a ransom."

Though my eyes were not opened, I had obtained mercy. The day would come when the Lord would answer for me in the day of my distress. He who restored the ring (or what it signified) promised to keep it. I later found unspeakable comfort in this —that I am not in my own keeping! "The Lord is my shepherd."

I know whom I have believed (see 2 Timothy 1:12). My Shepherd has won my trust. Satan still desires to have me so that he can sift me as wheat, but my Savior has prayed for me that my faith may not fail (see Luke 22:31). He is my security and power, my bulwark against which the gates of hell cannot prevail. But for this, many times since my first deliverance, I would have ruined myself. I fall. I stumble. I would have perished if His faithfulness had not been active in my behalf. He is my Sun and Shield, even unto death (see Psalm 84:11). "Bless the Lord, O my soul."

Nothing very remarkable occurred during the remainder of the voyage. I returned home in December 1743, and soon went again to Kent. I stayed there too long again and disappointed my father so greatly that he almost disowned me.

Before anything suitable in the way of vocation opened up for me, I was caught by the military after another piece of foolishness on my part and put on board a tender. Military tensions were aggravated by the presence of the French fleets off the English coasts. My father was not able to procure my release.

In a few days I was transferred to the ship *Harwich*, where I entered an entirely new scene of life. I endured a great deal of hardship for about a month.

My father decided then that I should remain in the navy, as war was expected daily. He procured a recommendation to the captain who elevated me to midshipman. I now had an easier life and, had my behavior been different, might have gained respect from my superiors. Instead, I met with companions who completed the ruin of my morals. Outwardly I looked conservative and polite, but inwardly my delight and habitual practice was wickedness.

My chief friend was a genial young man with few scruples. He knew how to argue me down

19

and impress me with his opinions in the most plausible way. He was fun to be with.

He was interested in the few books I had, and I was eager enough to show him how well-read I was. He soon perceived that I still had standards he had not broken down, and he began on a program to gain my confidence. He spoke rather favorably of religion at first. Then he began to undermine my attachment to the *Characteristics*, by Lord Shaftesbury. He argued with me and convinced me that I never had understood it in the first place. He soon convinced me, and I went his way with all my heart. I guess I was like the unwary sailor who leaves port just as a storm is rising. I renounced the hopes and comforts of the gospel at the very time when every other comfort was about to fail me.

Later, on a voyage to Lisbon, my friend was in a ship caught by a violent storm. The vessel and people escaped, but a great wave broke on board, sweeping him into eternity.

In December 1744 the *Harwich* was in harbor, but scheduled for a trip to the East Indies. The captain gave me liberty to go on shore for a day. Ignoring the consequences, I rented a horse and raced to take a last leave of the one I loved. I knew all the time I was there that I was getting more and more deeply in trouble back at the ship. The short time I stayed with her passed like a dream. On New Year's day I returned to the ship. I begged the captain to excuse my absence—which he did—but, since this wasn't the first stunt I had pulled, I lost his confidence for good!

When we did sail, we moved out of harbor with a very large fleet. The following night, several ships were lost, trying to get out to sea. A storm from the south had struck the coasts of Cornwall. The darkness of the night and the close proximity of so many vessels caused a great deal of confusion and damage. Our ship, though several times in imminent danger of being run down by other vessels, escaped unhurt. So many ships suffered that we had to put back to Plymouth.

While we were there, I learned that my father had come down to a city nearby. He had a connection at that time with another shipping company, and I thought that if I could just get to him, he might be able to secure a position for me on another ship that would be better than pursuing a long, uncertain voyage on the *Harwich* to the East Indies.

It was a principle of my life at that time that I would never think twice about anything I wanted to do. The thought had hardly occurred to me before I resolved to leave the ship—no matter what it cost. I did so in a typically foolish way.

I was sent in a boat one day to take care that none of the other people deserted. But I betrayed my trust and went off myself. I didn't know what road to take and didn't dare ask, for fear of being suspected a deserter. I had some general idea of the country and guessed right. I traveled for a number of miles and then found, on inquiry, that I was on the road to Dartmouth.

All went smoothly that day and part of the next. I was about two hours' walk from my father when

I was met by a small party of soldiers. I could not avoid or deceive them; they knew I was a deserter. They walked me back to Plymouth, guarding me like a criminal. I was embarrassed, and full of shame and very real fear. They confined me in the guardhouse for two days before sending me back on board my ship, where I was kept in irons at first and then stripped and whipped in front of everybody. Finally, I was degraded from my office.

All of my former companions were forbidden to show me the least kind of consideration. They could not even speak to me. As a midshipman, I'd had some authority, which I had not been reluctant to exercise. But now that I had been brought down to a level with the lowest, I became the butt of everyone's jokes.

If my present situation was bad, my future was worse. The officers and my former shipmates who had been my friends found it impossible to protect me from the abuse I had coming. They and I knew that they ran a risk of insubordination if they offered comfort to a man under discipline. On several occasions the captain showed me how furious he was with me—and the voyage was to last for five years!

I was totally miserable. Every hour brought some new insult and hardship, with no hope of relief or softening and no friend to take my part or listen to my complaints. And worse, nothing I felt or feared distressed me so much as to know I was being torn away from the one I so dearly loved. Should she ever learn of the manner of my going it would be doubtful that I could return with any hope of her being mine.

I could see nothing but darkness and misery. I

am sure that no one, except one whose conscience has been wounded by the wrath of God, could feel more dreadful than I did. I cannot express the wistfulness and regret with which I cast my last look on the English shoreline. I kept my eyes fixed on it until it disappeared. When I could see it no longer, I was tempted to throw myself overboard, ending all my sorrows at once.

But the secret hand of God restrained me.

# Letter 4

## My First Voyage to Africa

My dear Haweis:

You have asked for a more explicit account of my courtship. Let me tell you how it stood at the time I left England.

When Mary's family discovered that I had sincere interests in their daughter, no one considered it seriously. It served for tea-table talk among our friends, and nothing further was expected from it. But when after two years my desire for her had not lessened, and especially as it provoked me to act rather impetuously, her family began to consider the seriousness of my intentions. They were quite conscious of the coolness that still existed between their family and my father, and they rightly discerned that my father had not been consulted.

When I said my last good-bye, her mother told me, with as much affection as if I had been her own child, that she had no objections—that when both of us were older, there might be a very real probability that her daughter and I could get together. But as things stood then, she thought she should interfere. She said she did not want me to come back unless her daughter was away from home. That would be the case until I either gave up my intentions or assured her that I had my father's express consent to go on with our courtship.

It was all so difficult. Mary was young, gay, and quite naive in matters of love. She did not encourage me or refuse me, but I found her always on guard. She knew she had power over me, and she was clever enough to make proper use of it. She would neither understand my hints nor give me time to make a direct explanation. She told me years later that, from the moment she discovered my regard for her, the thought had been agreeable to her; she had often had an impression she could not account for that sooner or later she would be mine.

Let me return now to my voyage. All my old melancholy returned. Although I knew I deserved all the punishment I had received, and that the captain would have been justified in punishing me even more, I felt in my heart that I had been grossly injured. This worked so against my pride and wicked heart that I actually made plans to take the captain's life. That was one reason I was willing to prolong my own. Sometimes I was divided between which of the two I would do—take his life or take my own.

I was capable of anything. I hadn't the least fear of God, nor the least sense of conscience. I was sure that after death I would merely cease to be. All my troubles would be over. But some days I would have better thoughts. A ray of hope would come in, although I doubted that I would ever see better days or return to England to marry my Mary.

My love was the only restraint I had left. I could not bear the idea that she might think bad thoughts of me when I was dead. That single thought, which oddly had not held me back from a thousand smaller evils, proved to be the only thing preventing me from trying to kill the captain.

How long I could have continued fighting this battle, I do not know. But the Lord, whom I little thought of, knew my danger and was even then providing for my deliverance.

While I was still in Plymouth, I determined two things: one, that I would not go to India, and two, that I would go to Guinea. That turned out to be the Lord's will for me; but He accomplished both His way, not mine.

We had been at Madeira for some time. The business of the fleet was completed, and we were to sail the following day. On that memorable morning I stayed late in bed. I would have slept even longer, but one of the midshipmen—an old companion—came down and half joking and half seriously told me to get up. When I did not leap to obey his order, he cut the hammock down. I was angry, but I didn't dare let him know it.

It was strange that this person who made no profession of knowing why he did what he did was the one distinct messenger of God's provision for my needs. I said nothing further to him and went up on deck. That moment I saw a man putting his clothes into a boat. He told me he was leaving ship. When I asked him why, he said that two men from a ship from Guinea had asked to be transferred to the *Harwich*. The commodore of the fleet, Sir George Pocock, had ordered my captain to send two from our ship to take their place.

At once, I saw my chance. I begged that the boat would be detained for a few minutes and ran to the lieutenant. I pleaded with him to intercede with the captain that I might be the second man. Though I had been on poor terms with these officers and had disobeyed them at every turn, they did pity me and consented to allow me to transfer. In little more than half an hour from my awakening in my hammock, I was discharged from serving aboard the *Harwich* and was safely installed on board another ship.

That was one of the many critical turns in my life in which the Lord was pleased to show His concern for me by causing totally unexpected circumstances to concur in almost an instant of time. He did this several times, and each time brought me into an entirely new scene of action. Each incidence was usually delayed to almost the very last moment in which it could have taken place.

The ship I boarded was bound for Sierra Leone and the adjacent parts of what is called the Windward Coast of Africa. My new commander was acquainted with my father, and he received me very kindly. I believe he would have been my friend if I had acted in any kind of decent manner. But I had not yet learned my lesson. In fact, I acted much worse than I did on board the *Harwich*. I remember that when I was in the dinghy passing from one ship to the other I was really rejoicing in the exchange. I was going to live the life I pleased, without any control. From that time on, I became totally corrupt. Not only did I sin, but I got others to sin with me.

One natural result of my corruption was that I lost the good opinion of my new captain—not that he was at all religious or that he disliked my wickedness. But I became careless and disobedient. I didn't please him, because I didn't want to please him. And because he was a man with an odd temper, we easily disagreed. Besides, I had a clever streak that got me into more trouble every time I indulged it.

Once I imagined that he had insulted me, and I made up a song in which I ridiculed his ship, his intentions, and his person. I taught it to the whole ship's company and made him a laughingstock. I was that kind of ungrateful person. Of course, he knew all about the song and who composed it.

I went on like that for about six months. As our ship was preparing to leave the coast, our captain died. I was not on much better terms with his mate who now succeeded to the command. He had been mean to me before, and I had no doubt that if I went with him to the West Indies he would put me on board a man-of-war. And that, from what I had heard, was more dreadful than death. To avoid it, I knew I would have to remain in Africa.

One other man I knew of had arrived on this coast in very much the same condition. He had gone into the business of purchasing slaves from up-country and selling them to the ships at an advanced price. He had recently been in England and was returning on the ship I was in. He owned one-fourth of it.

His example impressed me with hopes that I could do the same. I arranged with him to come and work and, on that agreement, obtained my discharge from the ship. I did not take the precaution of prearranging the terms of my employment. I merely trusted his generosity. And I received no payment from the captain of the ship for my services. He just gave me a bill, which I could present to the owners of the ship when I got back to England. It was never paid, because the company went bankrupt before I could return.

The day the vessel sailed, I landed on the island of Benanoes with little more than the clothes on my back. It was as if I had escaped a shipwreck.

# Letter 5

## Trials in West Africa

My dear Haweis:

The following two years seem like an absolute blank. Since the hour of the Lord's grace to me was not yet come, I went deeper and deeper into wickedness, the way the heart of man always does when left to itself (see Jeremiah 17:9). Actually, looking back on those experiences now, I see the mercy of the Lord in banishing me to that remote land at a time when I was big with mischief, like a person diseased and very capable of spreading the infection wherever I went.

Had I been in England among my own countrymen, my wickedness would have had far greater scope. Out in Africa, I came into touch with only a few people and could do them little harm. The few I did have to talk with were too much like myself, and I soon sank too low to have any kind of influ-

31

ence at all. During the first year of my residence among them, some slaves thought themselves too good to speak to me.

The appointed time for the Lord to rescue me from myself was not until long after this. Only by His grace did I not lose my mind at this time. The sufferings I endured did slow down my rush to sin, and for this reason I count them among my blessings.

You would probably be interested in the country I was now confined to. The places I frequented at that time in my life became the locale in which I conducted my trade later. Actually, I would do business in the same places and with the same people who were then considering me on a level with their lowest slaves.

From Cape de Verd, the most western point of Africa, to Cape Mount, the whole coast is full of rivers. The main ones are the Gambia, the Rio Grande, the Sierra Leone, and the Sherbro. I was never on the Gambia, but the Rio Grande is quite familiar to me. Like the Nile, it divides into many branches near the sea. On the most northern, called the Cacheo, the Portuguese have a settlement. The most southern branch, known by the name of Rio Nuna, was the boundary line beyond which white men did not go to trade. The Sierra Leone territory is a mountainous peninsula, uninhabited and inaccessible because of the thick jungle that comes down to the waterline.

The Sherbro river is large and navigable. Just over forty miles to the southeast are three islands called the Benanoes. The perimeter around all three is about twenty miles. This is the center of the white men's residential colony. Some twenty-four miles in the same direction lie the Plantanes, three small islands just two miles off the coast where the Sherbro meets the sea. This river is more like an ocean sound, because several large rivers join it there. The most southern of these has a very peculiar course, running almost parallel to the coast, sometimes not more than a half mile distant.

My new master had formerly resided near Cape Mount. More recently he settled at the Plantanes on the largest of the three islands. It is a low, sandy island, about two miles in circumference and almost covered with palm trees.

We immediately began to build a house and to enter upon our trade. I had a real desire to make something of myself, since I had lost so much time. I am sure I would have gotten along very well with my new employer had he not turned against me. He was wound around the finger of a black woman who lived with him as a wife. She was a person of some consequence in her own country, and he knew he owed his prosperity initially to her. For some reason, she took an instant dislike to me. What made things worse was that I succumbed to a severe illness soon after I got there—before I had any chance to show him what I could do for him in his business.

I was still sick when he left on a trip to Rio Nuna, leaving me in this woman's hands. At first, she took care of me; but when I failed to recover soon, she grew weary and neglected me completely. I could not even get a glass of cold water from anyone when I was burning with fever. My bed was a mat spread on a chest. A log of wood was my pillow.

When my fever left me and my appetite returned, no one gave me anything to eat. She lived high, but she hardly gave me enough to sustain my life. Now and then when she was feeling superior, she would send me food from her own plate after her dinner. So greatly had I been humiliated that I received this with thanks and eagerness—as a beggar does a penny.

Once she even called me into her house to receive this from her own hand, but I was so weak and feeble that I dropped the plate. People who have plenty cannot imagine what that does to one in my condition. And she was cruel enough to laugh at my chagrin. Though the table was covered with dishes, she refused to give me any more food.

At times, I would be so ravenous that I would go out at night and pull up roots in the plantation, at the risk of being punished as a thief. I would eat them raw on the spot, for fear someone would see me. Boiled or roasted, those roots are delicious. Raw, they taste like potatoes.

Occasionally, strangers and even some of the slaves would slip crumbs to me from their own meager handouts. They would have been punished if anyone had seen them.

To make matters worse, this woman would sometimes pay me a visit—not to pity or comfort me, but to insult me. She would call me worthless and lazy and compel me to get up and walk—which I could hardly do. She would then get her slaves to mimic my motion, clap their hands, laugh, and throw limes at me. If they chose to throw stones, she didn't stop them. All of her slaves were required to take part in humiliating me; but once she was out of sight, even the lowliest of them pitied me.

Finally, my employer returned. I complained of the treatment his woman had given me, but he would not believe it. And, since she was within earshot, she made sure I got no better treatment.

On his second voyage, my master took me with him. We did pretty well for a while until a brother trader he met in the river persuaded him that I was unfaithful and stole his goods in the night or when he was on shore.

That was the only vice I could not be justly charged with. I was honest, if nothing else. I had always been faithful with the things he had put in my charge, even though I had every reason to get even with him for the way his woman had treated me. But he believed the charge made against me and condemned me without evidence.

From that time on he never trusted me out of his sight. When he left the ship, he would lock me up with only a pint of rice for my day's allowance. If he stayed longer, I had no relief until he returned. I would have starved if I had not been able to catch a few fish. When birds were killed for his dinner, I often got some of the entrails to use for bait. About the time of the changing of the tides, when the current was still, I would fish. And I often caught something. I cannot tell you what joy I felt when I caught a fish on my hook. Such a fish, hastily broiled, or rather half-burned, without sauce, salt, or bread, often gave me a delicious meal. If I caught nothing, I would sleep my hunger away until the slack water returned. Then I would try again.

My clothes were threadbare—what clothes they were. I had a shirt, a pair of trousers, a cotton handkerchief—instead of a cap—and about two yards of cotton cloth to wrap around me. With no more than that, I have been exposed to up to forty hours of incessant rains and gales of winds without the least shelter when my master was on shore.

I developed violent pains, which still bother me years later. The excessive cold and wet that I endured so soon after I had recovered from my long sickness not only broke my physical health, but broke my spirit. Better days later picked up my spirits; but it has taken years to overcome the effects of my physical breakdown.

About two months later we returned to the Plantanes. The rest of the time I was with that master was spent on that island. My haughty heart had been brought down completely. I had lost the fierceness that fired me on board the *Harwich*. But, looking back, I can see that I was no more changed than a tiger is tamed by hunger. Remove the trial, and I would be as wild as ever.

Strangely enough, I could collect my mind and do mathematical studies in the midst of all that. I had bought Barrow's *Euclid* at Plymouth. It was the only volume I had brought on shore when I joined this new employer. It was always with me. I used to take it to remote corners of the island by the seashore and draw my diagrams with a long stick on the sand. That way I often calmed my sorrows and almost forgot my feelings of anger and hatred. Without any other assistance, I mastered the first six chapters of *Euclid*.

# Letter 6

## My New Master

My dear Haweis:

Jacob made a statement that haunts me. Running from Esau, he had crossed the Jordan River. Years later, when returning home, he said, "With my staff I passed over this Jordan, and now I am become two bands."

That was my experience, for, during the mournful days to which my last letter refers, I was put to work planting lime and lemon trees. The plants I put in the ground were no taller than a young gooseberry bush.

Walking by, my employer and his mistress paused to watch what I was doing.

"Who knows?" he remarked. "By the time these trees grow up and bear, you may go home to England, obtain the command of a ship, and return to

39

reap the fruits of your labors. We see strange things happen sometimes."

He meant that as cutting sarcasm. I believe he thought it as probable that I should live to be king of Poland. Yet it did prove to be a prediction; when I did return from England as a ship's captain, I did pluck some of the first limes from those very trees.

What a contrast my life is now to the way it was then. I used to creep out in the dead of night to wash my one shirt on the rocks. I would put it on wet so that it would dry while I slept. When a ship's boat came to the island, I would hide in the woods, ashamed to be seen by strangers. And had you known, my friend, that my conduct, my principles, and my heart were still darker than my outward condition, you would marvel more at God's providential care and goodness.

I simply cannot get over the transformation He accomplished when He made me acceptable to Himself in the Beloved. He gave me friends who love me in spite of my past. He protected and guided me through a long series of dangers. I owe it to Him that I am still alive and that I am not still living in hunger, thirst, and nakedness. He delivered me and brought me to an easier life. I know many of His people. I am a friend of several of His most honored servants. I have an experimental knowledge of the power of His gospel. It is as difficult to count up my present privileges as it is to fully describe the evils and miseries of my past life that contrast with them.

I don't know exactly how long things continued in that unhappy state. I believe it was nearly a year. During that time I wrote to my father two or three times, giving him an account of my location and circumstances. I wanted him to help me. I told him that I would not return to England unless he wanted me to come and would send for me.

I also have letters I wrote to the one I loved. At my lowest point I still retained a hope of seeing her again.

My father did speak to a friend of his in Liverpool. That man gave orders to a captain of his own who was even then fitting out a ship bound for Gambia and Sierra Leone.

Within the year, as I have said, I obtained my master's consent to live with another trader on the same island. Without his consent I could not have made the switch. He had been unwilling to let me go earlier, but he changed his mind.

That move was certainly an advantage for me. I was soon decently clothed. I lived in plenty. I was considered a useful companion, and my new employer trusted me with the care of all his household effects, valued at $5,000—a significant investment at that time.

That man had several white servants and factories in different places, particularly one along the Kittam, the river which runs along the seacoast. He soon appointed me to go there, giving me a share in managing his business. Another of his servants lived with me and shared my responsibilities. We did as we pleased, business flourished, and our employer was satisfied.

I even began to think myself happy.

You know, there is a phrase we used in those

41

parts to describe such a happiness. We would say the white man has "grown black." It's not a matter of skin color, but of disposition. I've known several men who have settled in Africa after they've turned thirty or forty and who have let the life of the place gradually color their view of life, their customs, and even their patriotism. They've grown to prefer Africa to their own country. They've even adopted all the religious nonsense of the blacks and put more trust in amulets and divinations of the primitives than the wiser natives do.

I was finding that a sense of that infatuation with things black was growing on me. In time, perhaps, I might have yielded to that way of life. I had not lost my ties to England, of course, but the fact that I had no hope of ever getting home again made me willing to remain where I was. It was a way of coping with that disappointment.

But isn't that like the Lord? As soon as I had fixed that way of thinking in my mind, He purposed to break that mental set in pieces and deliver me from ruin in spite of myself.

The ship that had orders to bring me home arrived at Sierra Leone. The captain asked about me there and when he put in at the Benanoes. Someone told him I was a great distance away in the country, and he thought no more about me. But surely the hand of God had placed me at Kittam at just that time. If I had been at the Plantanes, I would not have heard of the ship until she had sailed on. The same thing would have been true if my new master had sent me to any other factory of his. At Kittam, I was only a mile from the seacoast.

I was at that very time just about to go inland, some distance from the sea, on a matter of trade. I had planned to set out a day or two before, but we decided to wait for a few things we needed that the next ship arriving would probably bring. My friend and I used the time to walk on the beach, where we would see any ship that passed by. I admit it was a remote hope, since not many ships put into that particular place to trade.

Sometime in February 1747—I don't know the exact day—my fellow servant saw a vessel sailing past and lit a fire to tell the captain we were interested in trade. He had already passed beyond the place, because he had a good wind. Half an hour later, he would have not seen the signal. But he threw out his anchor at that point, and my friend, using a canoe, went on board.

One of the first questions the captain asked my friend concerned me. When he learned I was so near, he came on shore himself to deliver his message.

Had an invitation from home reached me when I was sick and starving at the Plantanes, I would have considered it life from the dead. But now, for the reasons I have already told you, I did not care as much.

The captain, having found me, did not want to lose me. So he made up a story about having misplaced a large packet of letters and papers addressed to me. Those would have explained what he now was going to tell me, he said. Apparently, a person had recently died and left me a lot of money. The captain said that he had orders to pay up to the amount of half his cargo if it cost that to redeem me from my present indebtedness to my master. Everything he said was false, I learned later.

I thought over what he was telling me. My father's care for me and desire to see me was not enough to make me want to leave. But memories of my loved one, the hope of seeing her again, and the possibility that by accepting this offer I might once more be in a position to win her consent to marry me—this convinced me.

The captain further promised—and he did keep his word about this—that I would live in his cabin, eat at his table, and be his constant companion without having to do any work to pay for it.

Once again, I was suddenly freed from a captivity of about fifteen months. One hour before, I'd had no thought of making the change. I took him up on his offer at once, gathered my few belongings, and went on board. In a few hours I was far away from Kittam.

So blind and stupid was I at that time that I never thought twice about it. "Like a wave of the sea driven with the wind and tossed" (James 1:6), I was governed by present appearances and never looked further. But the One who is eyes to the blind was leading me in a way I knew not—the same way He has worked in the lives of countless others.

How many small events in the life of Joseph had such an influence on the small one following? If he had not dreamed, he would not have told his dream. If the Midianites had passed a day sooner or a day later, he would not have landed in Egypt. If they had sold him to any person but Potiphar, if his mistress had been a better woman, or if Pharaoh's officers had not displeased their lord, all that followed would have been different. The promises and purposes of God concerning Israel—the bondage, deliverance, wanderings and eventual settlement in the Promised Land—all seem to have hinged on the exact timing of the preceding events. If history had not been as it was—according to God's plan—then the promised Savior would not have appeared. Mankind would have remained in its sins, without hope. The counsels of God's eternal love would have been defeated.

We find a connection between Joseph's first dream, the history of the Jews, and the death of our Lord Christ—all glorious sequences of great and small events. What a comfort it is to know that, despite all the interference of men and nations in their attempts to frustrate any kind of righteous testimony on earth, the Lord has one constant design. From the foundation of the world He has planned the complete salvation of His people. He has been wise and strong and faithful to make even those things which opposed His design to be the things that promoted it.

# Letter 7

## Dangers and
## Deliverances

My dear Haweis:

Let me tell you about the next ship I was on. This time I was a passenger, with no assignments to keep me busy.

Our trade was collecting gold, ivory, dyers' wood, and beeswax. It takes much longer to collect a cargo like that than it does to pick up slaves. The captain had begun trading at Gambia four or five months before I came on board. He continued for a year more after I was with him. We ranged the whole coast as far as Cape Lopez, which lies about one degree south of the equator. We went more than a thousand miles farther from England than the place where I embarked.

To keep myself occupied, I sometimes turned to

my mathematics. Except for that, my life was one of continued godlessness and profanity. I do not know that I have ever met a man with a more vile mouth than mine. I wasn't even content with the common oaths everyone knew. I invented new ones every day—some so vivid that the captain, a blasphemer himself, would bawl me out.

From what I told him of my past adventures and from what he saw of my present conduct—especially as the voyage neared its end—the captain was sure he had gotten a Jonah on board. He was sure a curse went with me wherever I went and that all the troubles he had were because I was on board.

One of them I brought on myself.

Although I went to excess in almost every other extravagant sin, I never drank. My father often said that he knew I would eventually get my head on straight, as long as I continued avoiding liquor. But sometimes, just for fun, I would get a drinking contest going.

The last time I did that was when we were on the river Gabon. Four or five of us one evening sat down on deck to see who could hold out the longest, drinking geneva and rum alternately. A large seashell was our glass.

I was totally unfit for a challenge like this, because I could not stomach liquor at all. However, I offered the first toast, which I remember was a curse on the man who would start first! My brain was soon on fire, and I rose and danced around the deck like a maniac. In the process my hat went overboard. In the moonlight I could see the ship's dinghy nearby, and I started to throw myself over the side to get into it. In my flight I saw that the boat was not as close as I thought—perhaps some twenty feet from the ship's side. I was half over and would in a split second have plunged into the water when somebody caught hold of my clothes behind and pulled me back.

It was an amazing escape. I could not swim —even when I was sober. The tide was now running strong, and my companions were too drunk to save me. The rest of the ship's company was asleep. I was a split second away from death. I would have gone into eternity under the weight of my own curse.

Another time at Cape Lopez some of us shot a buffalo or wild cow in the jungle. We brought part of it on board and carefully marked (we thought) where the carcass was. That night we returned to get it, everyone following my lead. But night came on before we reached the place, and we lost our way. Sometimes we were in swamp water up to our waists; and when we reached dry land, we couldn't tell whether we were walking toward the ship or wandering farther away. Every step made us even more uncertain.

The night grew darker. We were caught in thick jungle where, perhaps, no one had ever been before. We were thoroughly scared, because no one had thought to bring a light or food or any kind of gun. We expected a tiger to rush out from behind every tree. Clouds blotted out the stars, and we had no compass to tell us which direction to take.

Thank God, no beast attacked us. After several hours the moon rose, showing us which direction was east. We saw at once that we had been going farther away from the seaside. We turned around and went east. Even after we got to the water's edge, we found we were a long way from the ship. Finally, we made it, frightened and terribly tired, but unharmed.

Those and a number of other deliverances were all lost on me. My conscience had ceased altogether. Years had gone by since I'd had any sense of conscience at all. The times I was near death from sickness, I didn't have the least concern about the consequences, should I succumb. I seemed to have passed the point of no return—neither God's judgments nor His mercies had even the slightest impression on me.

We finally finished our business at Cape Lopez and, after a few days' layover at the island of Annabona to get provisions, we started home. We left in January 1748. From Annabona to England, without touching any port in between, was about seven thousand miles, because we had to follow trade winds.

First, we sailed eastward until we were near the coast of Brazil. Then we turned northward to the banks of Newfoundland. There, after a totally uneventful trip, we stopped half a day to fish for cod. That was only to change the pace, because we already had enough provisions. Little did we expect that those fish would be all we later would have to eat.

We left the banks March 1 with a hard westerly wind that pushed us fast toward home. I became more and more uncomfortable about the condition of the ship. Because we had been in a hot climate for so long, she was out of repair and really unfit for stormy weather. The sails and ropes were worn, among other things.

On March 9, the day before our catastrophe, I happened to pick up Stanhope's book on Thomas à Kempis to pass the time. I read it casually, as if it were a novel. However, this time a thought rose in my mind—*What if those things are true?* The thought was too much for me, and I soon shut the book. My conscience goaded me once more, but I decided that, whether those things were true or not, I would take the consequences of the way I had already chosen. I put an end to that kind of thinking by joining in the first conversation that came my way.

But the Lord's time was come, and the conviction I was so unwilling to receive was deeply impressed on me. I went to bed that night feeling as secure and indifferent to God as I had ever been. I was awakened later from a sound sleep by the force of a violent storm that had broken on us. Many of the pounding waves came below decks and filled the cabin where I lay. I heard a cry from on deck that the ship was going down. I rushed to the ladder, where I met the captain, who told me to get a knife.

While I returned for the knife, another person went up in my place and was instantly washed overboard. We hardly had time to give him a second thought. The sea had torn away the upper timbers on one side and wrecked the ship in a matter of minutes. It was a miracle that any of us survived.

We went to the pumps, but the water increased, in spite of all our efforts. The captain sent some of us to bail in another part of the ship with buckets and pails. We were only eleven or twelve people doing this, and we soon found that the ship was almost full. With an ordinary cargo, she would have sunk. But we had a large quantity of beeswax and wood on board, and those were lighter than the water. And since we received the damage to the ship in the very teeth of the gale, as it subsided we were able to use clothes and bedding to stop the leaks. Over those we nailed boards, and immediately the water aboard seemed to go down.

As we pumped hard, I tried to cheer my companions. I told one of them that in a few days all that would be left of the experience would be the stories we would tell over a glass of wine. But he was a less hardened sinner than I, and he replied with tears, "No, it is too late now."

About nine o'clock, being cold and tired, I went to speak with the captain. But he was busy elsewhere. As I returned to the pumps, I said, almost without any meaning, "If this will not do, the Lord have mercy on us." That sentence, although spoken just casually, was the first desire I had breathed for mercy for many years. I was instantly struck with my own words. *What mercy could there be for me?* I thought.

I returned then to the pump and remained there until noon. Almost every passing wave broke over my head, but we had tied ourselves to the ship with ropes so that we would not be washed overboard. I fully expected that each time the ship went down in a trough she would never rise again. I dreaded death now. In my heart I knew that if the Scriptures I had long since opposed were true, I deserved the worst.

Still, I was only half convinced, and I remained for quite some time in a sullen frame of mind, half despair and half impatience. I thought that, if the Christian religion was true, I could not be forgiven. I was expecting—at times almost wishing—to know the worst that would happen to me. I fully expected to perish any minute.

# Letter 8

## Voyage Homeward

My dear Haweis:

March 21 is a day I will always remember. In fact, I have observed it every year since 1748. On that day the Lord delivered me out of deep waters.

I continued at the pump from three in the morning until near noon. And then, because I could do no more, I went and lay down on my bed, not sure —and almost not even caring—if I would ever rise again.

In about an hour's time I was called. In no condition to pump, I went to the helm and steered the ship till midnight, except for a short time for supper.

While standing there, I had time to ponder the religious life I had once lived, as well as the warnings and deliverances I had met with since. I thought of the vile course of my life and particularly of the way I had made fun of the gospel. I knew that there could never have been such a sinner as myself. I knew my sins were too great to be forgiven.

Interestingly, Scriptures I had known long before began to return to my memory. I thought particularly of those awful passages in Proverbs 1:

> Because I have called, and ye refused; I have stretched out my hand, and no man regarded; but ye have set at nought all my counsel, and would none of my reproof: I also will laugh at your calamity; I will mock when your fear cometh; when your fear cometh as desolation, and your destruction cometh as a whirlwind; when distress and anguish cometh upon you. Then shall they call upon me, but I will not answer; they shall seek me early, but they shall not find me: for that they hated knowledge, and did not choose the fear of the LORD: They would none of my counsel: they despised all my reproof. Therefore shall they eat of the fruit of their own way, and be filled with their own devices. [Proverbs 1:24-31]

And the verses in Hebrews and 2 Peter also seemed to fit my case and character exactly.

> For it is impossible for those who were once enlightened, and have tasted of the heavenly gift, and were made partakers of the Holy Ghost, and have tasted the good word of God, and the powers of the world to come, if they shall fall away, to renew them again unto repentance; seeing they crucify to them-

selves the Son of God afresh, and put him to an open shame. [Hebrews 6:4-6]

For if after they have escaped the pollutions of the world through the knowledge of the Lord and Saviour Jesus Christ, they are again entangled therein, and overcome, the latter end is worse with them than the beginning. [2 Peter 2:20]

It seemed that those verses proved that the Scriptures are inspired, because they so fit my situation. With that idea filling my mind, I waited in fear and anxiety for my inevitable doom.

Yet, though I thought that, actually I had no clear view of the infinite righteousness and grace of Jesus Christ my Lord. Several years later, my eyes were opened to recognize my true state, my nature, and my practice. I think if I had seen the greatness of His power that night, I would have been instantly overwhelmed and crushed like a moth.

When we heard about six in the evening that the ship was free of water, a gleam of hope rose in my heart. I thought I saw the hand of God in this, and I began to pray. I could not say the prayer of faith; I could not call Him "Father." I am sure the sound of my prayer in His ears was like wild birds calling.

I now began to think of that Jesus whose name had been a curse word on my lips. I remembered particulars of His life and death—a death for sins not His own, but for those who in their misery should put their trust in Him. I knew all that in my head, but now I wanted the evidence. I wasn't just

57

going to leap out in blind faith. I decided to read the Scriptures themselves for proof.

One of the first helps I received came from Luke 11:13—"If ye then, being evil, know how to give good gifts unto your children: how much more shall your heavenly Father give the Holy Spirit to them that ask him?" I knew that to profess faith in Christ when I did not believe He ever existed was no better than a mockery of the heart-searching God. But this verse spoke of a Spirit, who would be given to those who asked for Him.

I reasoned this way: *If this book is true, the promise in this passage must be true. I need that Spirit who wrote the whole Bible in order to understand it.* My intention was strengthened by another verse that came back into my mind: "If any man will do his will, he shall know of the doctrine, whether it be of God, or whether I speak of myself" (John 7:17). I decided that, even though I couldn't say from my heart that I believed the gospel, I would take its truth for granted for the present with the hope that, as I studied it more, I might become convinced.

Some people will say that I was trying to persuade myself of that opinion. And perhaps I was. But let me point out to them that they would, too, if God had shown them what He showed me on that ship. In the gospel I at least saw hope for my soul. On every other side all I saw was black, unfathomable despair.

The wind had not moderated, but it continued to push us steadily toward port. We were still in danger, but we were not as fearful as we had been—to say the least. Down below we found chaos. Anything that floated had been beaten to pieces by the violent motion of the ship. Our livestock—pigs, sheep, and poultry—had all been washed overboard in the storm. The only food we had was the fish we had caught on the banks and some food intended for hogs.

The sails, too, were mostly blown away. We were able to move, but only slowly when the wind was with us. We imagined we were about 350 miles from land, but in reality we were much farther.

My leisure time was spent reading and meditating on the Scriptures and praying to the Lord for mercy and instruction.

Things continued like this for four or five days, perhaps longer.

We awoke one morning to joyful shouts from the watch on deck that he saw land. We rushed up and saw a marvelously beautiful dawn. The light was just strong enough to reveal distant objects—a mountainous coast about twenty miles from us that dropped down in a cape or point. A little farther we could see two or three small islands rising out of the water. The appearance and position resembled what we were expecting—the northwest tip of Ireland. We whooped it up—sure that we would be in port the next day if the wind continued. The captain distributed the last of our brandy, and we finished up the last of our bread for joy at this welcome sight.

Then the mate, in grave tones, said that he wasn't too sure it was land, after all. If one of the common sailors had said as much, the rest of us would have beat him for raising such a doubt. But since it was the mate, we all just argued. The case was soon decided when one of our little islands began to grow red from the approach of the sun, rising just underneath it. We had been too hasty. Our land was nothing but clouds. In half an hour the whole scene had disappeared.

You cannot imagine how low our spirits sank, even though sailors have often been deceived by mirages. However, we comforted ourselves that land wasn't far off and that we would be there soon, if the wind held.

That very day our fair wind subsided, and the next morning a gale sprang up from the southwest, directly against us. It continued to blow for two weeks. The ship was so wrecked that we had to turn her to keep the wind always on the broken side. With the wind coming from that direction, we were driven still farther from our port. We were a long way west of Scotland and far out of the lane of traffic that might bring other ships to our rescue. We figured we were the first ship to be in that part of the ocean at that season of the year.

Our provisions were low. Half a salted cod was the only food for twelve people for a whole day. We had plenty of fresh water but not a drop of liquor, no bread, hardly any clothes, and very cold weather. We had to keep the pumps going incessantly to keep the ship above water. So much labor and so little food wasted us fast. One man died. Yet our sufferings were light compared to our fears.

We were scared we would either starve to death or fall so low that we would begin eating one another. Our hope grew dimmer every day.

It was then that a further trouble arose, aimed just at me. It seemed the captain, whose temper was soured by all we had gone through, got it into his head that I was the cause of all the trouble. He was certain that if I was thrown overboard, the rest of them would be saved from death. I'm sure he didn't plan to toss me over, but the constant repetition of this in my ears all day long made me feel uneasy—especially since my conscience told me that he was right. I thought it very probable that everything that had happened to us was on my account. God had at last decided to hold me accountable.

However, as we sailed along, I became far more hopeful. When we were ready to give up all hope of ever getting to shore, the wind came about to the very point we had been hoping for. We could head our prow in the right direction and keep the broken part of the ship completely out of the water. As gently as our few remaining sails could bear it, we sailed until we once more saw land.

First, the island Tory appeared; the next day we anchored in Lough Swilly, Ireland. This was April 8, just four weeks after the great storm broke on us at sea. As we sailed into that port, our last remnants of food were boiling in the pot. We had not been there two hours when a great wind began to blow. If we had been at sea that night in our shattered condition, I know we would have gone to the bottom.

About this time, I began to *know* that there is a

God who hears and answers prayer. How many times He had delivered me!

And, yet, I was still not grateful or trusting enough to give Him my heart.

# Letter 9
## Religious Awakenings

My dear Haweis:

Before I continue, I would like to look back just a bit, to give you a clearer indication of what I was going through at this time. It is strange to me that —although I shared the pangs of hunger, the cold, the weariness, and the fears of sinking and starving with the other men on board—I was the only one to be struck with any sense of the hand of God, delivering us from danger.

Now, I know that unless the Lord Himself does the work, it just does not get done. The men with me were totally unaffected and soon even forgot what we had all gone through. I was no better or wiser than they, but the Lord was pleased to give me a particular mercy—I, the most unlikely person in the ship to receive it. Always before, I had hardened my heart whenever God seemed to be scolding me. I can give no reason at all for His mercy, except that it seemed good to Him to do.

There was no one on board that I could share these things with, no one from whom I could ask advice. As to books, I had a New Testament, the Stanhope book I've already mentioned, and a book of Bishop Beveridge's sermons. One on the crucifixion really affected me. I was also struck by the parable of the fig tree in Luke 13, the story of Saint Paul in 1 Timothy 1, and—particularly—the account of the prodigal son in Luke 15. I felt that no one more perfectly fit the picture of the prodigal than myself. The goodness of the father in not only receiving, but in running to meet such a son—an illustration of the Lord's goodness to returning sinners—really moved me.

I spent a lot of time in prayer during those days. The Lord had saved me physically, and I was depending on Him to keep it up. The circumstances we continued to experience helped make me more serious and earnest in crying to Him who alone could calm my heart. Sometimes I thought I would be willing to die of even starvation if I could be assured of being a believer. I could get no assurance. But before we arrived in Ireland I was sure in my own mind of the truth of the gospel and of the fact that it really fit my needs. I saw that the obedience and sufferings of Jesus Christ had actually allowed God to be not only merciful but just in pardoning sins. By that time, I really believed in the marvelous doctrine of God manifest in the flesh, reconciling the world to Himself.

I am glad that I had never heard those theologies

that say that Christ was merely an upper servant or, at most, a demigod. I needed a Savior, and I found one in the New Testament. The Lord had done a marvelous thing. I was no longer an infidel; I heartily renounced my former wickedness. Conscious of God's mercy in bringing me through all my dangers, I became more serious. I was sorry for my past misspent life, and I determined to reform myself. I was freed from the habit of swearing, once second nature to me. To all appearances, I was a new man.

I'm sure the Holy Spirit did this in me, using the power of God. But in some ways I didn't have the whole truth. I was certainly conscious of my enormous sins, but I had little consciousness of the fact that my heart was evil. I had no understanding of spiritual principles, or of the hidden life of a Christian who enjoys communion with God by Jesus Christ, depending on Him for hourly supplies of wisdom, strength, and comfort. I was still depending on my own ability to do better in the future.

I had no Christian friend or faithful minister to tell me that my own strength not to sin lacked as much as my own righteousness. I began to look for serious books, but since I did not know which ones were good, I often made wrong choices. I learned a lot from the Lord, little by little and often by painful experience. I was still surrounded by the same evil company as before, but I could no longer mock sin or joke about holy things. I did not question the truth of Scripture anymore or quench the rebukes my conscience gave me when I sinned. I consider this time the beginning of my return to God—or rather, of His return to me. But with the knowledge I now have, I am sure I was not a believer in the full sense of the word until some time later.

I have told you, Haweis, that all during the days of our trial we comforted ourselves that we had plenty of fresh water. Since most of our diet was salt fish and we had no bread, we all drank as much as we wanted, with no fear of running out. Only when we were safe in Ireland did we discover that five of the six large barrels of water were empty. They had sprung leaks when they were lifted out of their places by the violent movement of the ship when we were fighting that storm.

While the ship was being refitted at Lough Swilly, I went to Londonderry. I lodged with a good family, who treated me very kindly and cared for me so well that I soon recovered my health and strength. Twice a day I went to prayers at church. While I was there, I told the pastor I wanted to receive the sacraments at the next opportunity.

When the day arrived, I rose very early and carefully reminded the Lord in my private devotions that I was His forever, and only His. It was a sincere surrender—I lived up to all the knowledge I had—even though later, under the subtlety of Satan's temptations, I was seduced to forget those vows. But though my knowledge of gospel salvation was meager, that day I experienced a peace and satisfaction at the Lord's table that I had never known before.

The next day I went shooting with the mayor of the city and some other men. As I climbed up a steep bank, pulling my shotgun after me, it went off so near my face as to burn away the corner of my hat. When we think ourselves the safest, we can still be in as much danger as when our whole world is conspiring to destroy us. I realized I had to count on God to guard me, on land or sea.

During our stay in Ireland, I wrote home. The ship I was in had not been heard of for eighteen months and had been given up for lost long before. My father never expected to hear that I was alive. He had already made arrangements to leave London for a position as governor of York Fort in Hudson's Bay, Canada, and he never returned. He received my letter just a few days before he left. And then he sailed before I landed in England. He had wanted to take me with him, but God had planned otherwise. One hindrance after another delayed us in Ireland until it was too late.

I did receive two or three affectionate letters from him, but I never saw him again. Three years later, I expected to have the opportunity of asking his forgiveness for the pain my youthful disobedience had caused him. But the ship that was to have brought him home came without him.

Before he left England, he had paid a visit to my friends in Kent and had given his consent to the marriage that had been talked of for so long a time. So, when I returned, I found I had only the consent of one person to gain, and I felt as uncertain of that as on the first day I saw her.

I arrived at Liverpool the end of May 1748, about the same day my father sailed. But the Lord found me another father—the gentleman whose ship had brought me home. He received me with the greatest kindness and with strong assurances of friendship. He insisted on helping me in every way he could. Had the Lord not saved me on the way home, nothing this man could have done for me would have helped.

He even offered me the command of a ship, but I turned him down. I had been so unsettled and careless before, I thought I had better make another voyage first and learn to obey. I wanted also to gain experience in business before I agreed to shoulder the responsibility of an entire ship.

The mate of the ship I came home in was given command of a new ship, and I asked to go on board as mate to him.

I made a short visit to London, but had only one opportunity to see my Mary. I was always awfully clumsy in telling her just how I felt. So, after I returned to London, I wrote her a letter telling her exactly how I felt. Her answer, though cautious, satisfied me. She was not attached to anyone else and was willing to wait for me until the end of my new voyage.

# Letter 10

## Adventures as a Slave Dealer

My dear Haweis:

Have you ever stood on a point where you could see a number of sailing ships heading in to port? Sometimes standing on a dock at a marina you will get this same impression. All the boats coming in have a number of things in common—a compass to steer by, the port in view, and general rules of navigation that are the same for all the pilots.

They also differ. No two of them would meet the same proportion of wind and weather at the same moment. Others would have a favorable wind one minute and, just as they think they are almost home, the wind will shift. Some are really threatened by wind and wave, and just as they are about to go on the rocks, they escape and get home safely.

Some meet their greatest difficulties at first. They put out in a storm and are often beaten back. Finally, things calm down, and they go and come without further mishap. They return to port with a rich cargo. Some are hounded by enemy ships and must fight their way through. Still others have a routine voyage with nothing unexpected occurring.

Our lives as believers are just like that. Forgive my simile here. It's just that I have had a long time to think about such things. All true believers walk by the same rule and pay attention to the same things. The Word of God is their compass. The Lord Jesus is both their polar star and their sun of righteousness. Their hearts and faces are all set heavenward. They are one Body. One Holy Spirit lives in them. Yet their experiences, based on these same principles, are far from identical.

The Lord knows the situation, the temperament, and the talents of each one, as well as the particular services or trials He has appointed for him. Some pass through life more smoothly than others, but everyone is tried at times. But the One "who walketh upon the wings of the wind" (Psalm 104:3) and measures "the waters in the hollow of his hand" (Isaiah 40:12) will not allow anyone in His charge to perish in the storms—although some might at one time or another be ready to give up hope.

We must not make the experiences of others a rule binding us, nor make our own experiences a rule for others. My own history has been extraordinary. I do not think I have met a single person who has a testimony like mine. Very few have been retrieved from as wicked a state as I have lived in. Those that have been have come through deep conviction, and the Lord has given them peace and a future more zealous, bright, and inspiring than is commonly the case.

My own convictions were not as deep as I would have expected them to be—that is, the Lord could rightfully have taken me to the bottom and really "raked me over the coals." And my first steps of faith were as weak as you can think. I never knew that time of first love as mentioned in Jeremiah 2:2: "Go and cry in the ears of Jerusalem, saying, Thus saith the LORD, I remember thee, the kindness of thy youth, the love of thine espousals, when thou wentest after me in the wilderness, in a land that was not sown."

Or Revelation 2:4: "Nevertheless, I have somewhat against thee, because thou hast left thy first love."

You would think that after such a wonderful, unhoped-for deliverance as I had—after my eyes were opened a little to see things right—I would have immediately become a fanatic for the Lord and would, like Paul, have consulted no more with flesh and blood.

But that was not the case with me. I had learned to pray. I valued the Word of God. I was no longer a drunk, given over to every evil, but my soul still loved the dirt.

Soon after I left Liverpool when I shipped out, I began to grow lazy in my devotions. I joked around a lot, seeking a good time. My conscience got after me, but I refused to listen. My spiritual armor gone, I fell away fast. By the time I got to Guinea, I was living a life that would make anyone think I had forgotten all about the Lord's mercies. I was never profane; I did not take His name in vain. But my spiritual enemy prepared a table of temptations for me to feast on, and I became his easy victim. For about a month he rocked me to sleep, as I did things I would not have thought myself capable of anymore.

Sin first deceives, and then it hardens. I was not tightly chained, but I had no power to free myself —and little desire to. Sometimes I would think about the fix I had gotten into; if I tried to change my ways, I would just sink deeper.

I was just like Samson when he said, "I will go forth, and shake myself, as at other times." But the Lord had departed from him, and he felt helpless in the hands of his enemies. I often remember that time of my life—and how I am, even now, so weak in myself, not capable of standing a single hour without a continual, fresh supply of strength and grace from my heavenly Source.

Finally, the Lord, whose power and willingness to forgive are infinite, stepped in and called a halt. My business on that particular voyage was to sail from place to place to purchase slaves. I left my ship at Sierra Leone and went to Plantanes, the scene of my former captivity. Everyone there made a fuss over me, even those who used to despise me. The lime trees I had planted were growing tall and would bear fruit in one more year. I would come back with a ship of my own and pick their fruit, fulfilling my former master's prediction. Upon my return to this place, I fell sick with a high fever that put me flat on my back where God could reach me. He broke the pattern I was stuck in and brought me back to my senses.

My past dangers and deliverances, my anguished prayers when I was in trouble, my dead-serious vows before the Lord that day I sat at the Lord's table, and my wicked, ungrateful responses to Him for all His goodness to me—those things came to my mind at once. I began to wish I had gone overboard with the pigs and chickens when that North Atlantic storm hit us. And, at first, as God was now dealing with me again, I felt as if the door of hope for me was shut tight. But I knew better, and this feeling went away.

Weak and almost delirious, I got out of bed and crept to a secluded part of the island. There I had a freedom in prayer I had never had before. I made no more resolutions to be a better man. I simply cast myself on the Lord to do with me whatever He wanted. I did not have a shred of power to do anything right. All I could do was throw myself at His feet, receiving the good of Christ's death for me in a way I had never done before.

I prayed for His forgiveness and found the burden lifted from my conscience. Not only did my peace come back, but my health, too. It didn't happen instantly, but by the time I returned to the ship two days later, I was perfectly well before I got on board.

I mark that day as the turning point in my spiritual experience. I came into the good of being delivered from the power and dominion of sin—even though I still, to this day "groan, being burdened" with the effects and ever-present conflicts of my sin nature (see 2 Corinthians 5:4).

I began to wait on the Lord in prayer as I had never done before. And though I have often grieved His Spirit and wandered foolishly from Him since then, His power and grace have preserved me from any more black departures into a life of sin. I am humbly trusting His mercy and His promises to be with me as my Guide and Guard till the end of my life.

I spent my off-duty hours learning the Latin language, which I had entirely forgotten. I got the idea of doing that from a suggestion in one of Horace's poems that I read in a magazine. Only because of sheer hard work—I studied when I should have slept—was I able to make good progress in it before I returned to England. I not only understood the sense and meaning of many poems and epistles, but I began to appreciate the beauties of their composition and develop a real enthusiasm for the classics. Actually I felt I had more of Horace in my mind than some who are masters of the Latin language. I had so few books to turn to for help that I usually had a passage memorized before I even fully understood what it meant.

During the eight months we were trading up and down the coast, I was exposed to many dangers and perils from burning suns and chilling mists, winds, rains, and thunderstorms. I was in danger in open boats, on shore, and in the jungles—where cruel and treacherous natives were watching for any chance they could find to get even with us.

Several boats were intercepted. Some white men were poisoned. I buried six or seven of my own men with fevers. Going on shore or returning in the little canoes, I was more than once overturned by the violence of the surf. Each time someone rescued me and brought me in to land, half-dead. I didn't know how to swim.

I have many tales like this and many other stories I have forgotten. Let me tell you one, dear Haweis, that is typical of the rest.

When our trading was finished and we were about to sail to the West Indies to deliver our slaves, I had to go ashore for wood and water. We were then at Rio Cestors. I used to go into the river in the afternoon with the sea breeze, buy my cargo in the evening, and return to ship in the morning with the land wind. I had made several voyages like that before, although our boat was old and almost unfit for use.

I finished lunch with the captain, received his orders, and slid down the ropes into the boat alongside. I was just ready to let go, when the captain came up from his cabin and called me back on board again. I went, expecting that he would have further orders for me. But he said that I should remain on board. He ordered another man to go in my place. I was surprised at that. He had never done this before. I had always been on that boat when it went on such errands. I asked him why he was detaining me, and he could not even give me a reason. That was what he wanted, and that was that.

So the boat left without me—and never returned.

She sank that night in the river, and the person who had taken my place was drowned.

I was astonished when we learned the news the next morning. And the captain, who was a stranger to religion, was as astonished as I. He said that he had no other reason for calling me back, except that it came suddenly to his mind that I should not go.

# Letter 11

## Marriage

My dear Haweis:

A few days after my marvelous deliverance from death, our ship sailed for Antigua and then to Charleston in South Carolina. I knew there were many Christians in that place, but I did not know where to find them. I supposed that all who attended church were good Christians and that all who preached from pulpits were as well. I had two or three opportunities to hear a minister named Smith, who, from what I've learned since, was probably an excellent, powerful preacher of the gospel. But something in his manner struck me as strange, and I did not seem able to understand what he was saying.

The best words that men can speak often have no effect whatsoever until the Spirit of God explains them and applies them to the heart He has opened. During these days it seemed that the Lord wanted me to learn nothing more than what He enabled me to understand from my own experience and meditation.

My conduct as a young Christian was very inconsistent. Almost every day, when my business would permit, I would walk into the woods and fields and commune with God in prayer and praise. Yet, in the evenings, I would go along with men searching for amusement. I had no wish to take part; I was merely along to watch. My own interest in such foolishness was just not very keen anymore.

I simply did not at that time see any need for separation from the world and the worldly. I just went along with custom and with my companions. The Lord kept me from what I *knew* was sinful, and I had, for the most part, peace of conscience. My strongest desires were for the things of God.

Not understanding that I should "abstain from all appearance of evil" (1 Thessalonians 5:22), I often edged right up to the brink of temptation. But the Lord was gracious to me in my weakness and didn't allow the enemy of my soul to gain any ground against me. I was gradually shown how foolish and inconvenient those things were. I gave up one after another, as the Lord gave me strength. But it was some years before I was delivered from occasionally toying with many things I now don't let myself even consider.

Finally, we finished our voyage and arrived in Liverpool. When the ship's affairs were settled, I went to London and then, as you might expect, right on to Kent. More than seven years had gone by since my first visit. And now, by the overruling goodness of God, who had preserved me from my own stubborn passions, I was able to consummate what I had wanted all along. I had turned from my foolishness, and my interest in settling down patterned my life. Every obstacle was now removed. With friends on all sides consenting, the matter lay just between ourselves, and we were married February 1, 1750. I was twenty-five years old.

I want you to know, dear Haweis, that my marriage has been a very happy one. I am sure I appreciate it all the more because of the eight disagreeable years I went through before. If you look back over my letters, you will have to admit that few people have known more misery than I. I marvel that the Lord preserved me, because I could, at seventeen, have locked in on a way of life with no turning back. The Lord knew the timing. Had we married before the Lord changed my heart, we both would have been unhappy. I can quote David from a full heart, "Surely goodness and mercy [have followed] me all the days of my life" (Psalm 23:6).

But my heart was still hard and ungrateful to the God of my life. You would think that His great mercy in giving me the delights of my heart would be enough to lock me into a lifetime of obedience and praise. Instead, I rested in the gift and forgot the Giver. My heart was satisfied with things as they were, and I began to grow spiritually careless. Things started getting worse.

Fortunately for me, I received orders in June to

go to Liverpool. I would be getting back to work. But—wouldn't you know—now I didn't want to go. The pain of leaving my dear wife—not knowing how long I would be gone or if I would ever see her again—was too much. But the Lord strengthened me. I was a poor, weak, idol-loving man; but now I knew the way of access to the throne of grace by the blood of the Lord Jesus, and my heart rested in that.

And my God continued to work in my heart. He showed me His power for godly living and used this experience as an opportunity to make me more a man of prayer than before. My former ways were flat and tasteless to me now. I practiced self-denial, and the Lord blessed me.

While I was still in England, I wrote her daily. When I was at sea, I wrote two or three times a week, even though there was no way to mail any letters. Whenever we touched port, I would send them off. I now have nearly two hundred pages of that correspondence in my desk. Writing to her did me a lot of good, too. I had time to think and write to her about a number of different things. I developed an ability to write freely that I'd never had before. As I grew in the Lord, my letters became more serious. I still enjoy looking at what I wrote. The letters remind me of many times when the Lord worked in my life—incidents I might otherwise have forgotten.

I sailed from Liverpool in August 1750, as the commander of a good ship. I had a crew of thirty men and felt it important to treat them humanely and to be a good example for them. I ordered that we have public worship twice every Sunday, and I conducted the services myself.

I had a great deal of leisure time, so I studied Latin and did very well at it. Before two or three trips were done, I had become well-acquainted with the classics. I read Terence, Virgil, Cicero, Buchanan, Erasmus, and Cassimir. I thought of how great it would be to become a Latin scholar and write pure and elegant Latin.

I did write some essays, but the Lord had other things in mind for me. He drew me nearer to Himself and gave me a fuller view of the person of Christ, my "Pearl of great price," hidden for me in the field of His Holy Word. For this, I was quite willing to let go of my newly acquired Latin riches.

I began to think that my life was too short for that kind of play. Not one Latin poet or historian could tell me a word about the Lord Jesus, so I decided to study only those who could. I studied the classics for only one morning a week for a while and then stopped altogether. I now preferred George Buchanan's *Psalms* to a whole shelf of Elzevirs.

About this same time, for the same reason, I stopped studying math. Not only was I spending too much time with it, but my head was much too full of schemes and theorems. I was tired of cold truth that could neither warm me nor help my heart. I found no traces of this kind of wisdom in the life of the Lord or in the writings of Paul. I was "spending my labor for that which is not bread." The Lord set before me "wine and milk, without money and without price." That was enough for me.

My first voyage kept me away from home for fourteen months and led me through various dangers and difficulties. But nothing very remarkable happened. Even though this first time I had seen many fall on my right hand and on my left (see Psalm 91:7), the Lord brought me home in peace and in safety.

I got home on November 2, 1751.

# Letter 12

## Seafaring Life

My dear Haweis:

Between my first and second voyages, I began to
keep a diary—a habit I have since found very valuable. I was able to document my progress. I must
admit that I still had periods of ungratefulness and
evil in my heart. I found that a comfortable life,
surrounded by friends who waited on me hand and
foot, would not bring me closer to God. Yet, on the
whole, I did gain ground spiritually.

I was introduced to books that gave me more
insight into Christian doctrine and experience. I
particularly enjoyed Scougall's *Life of God in the
Soul of Man*, Hervey's *Meditations*, and *The Life of
Colonel Gardiner*.

I heard none but the ordinary kind of preaching,
and I had no close Christian friends. I was also held
back by my own cowardly reserve—still afraid of

what people would think of me. Though I could not live without prayer, I didn't even suggest to my wife that we pray together until she urged that we do it. You would think that a person who had been forgiven as much as I had would love the Lord more and be more on fire for Him.

But duty called again, and I sailed from Liverpool in a new ship in July 1752. A seafaring life certainly cuts a person off from public gatherings and communion with Christians, but it has the advantage of encouraging the life of God in the soul—especially if you have command of a ship. You are able to curb misbehavior in the lives of others, and you are able to set your own schedule. It is easier on these African trips, because ships carry a double crew of men and officers. That made my job very easy; and, except for the occasional hurry of trade on the African coast, I had a lot of leisure time.

I never cease to be amazed at the wide expanse of heaven and ocean that make up my world. And God continually amazes me with daily answers to prayer that strengthen my faith and make up for the advantages a religious sailor could enjoy only on shore. And even though my knowledge of spiritual things was then very small, I sometimes look back on that time with regret. I never knew sweeter hours of communion with my Lord than in my last two voyages to Guinea, both in the seclusion of my cabin on shipboard and among the Africans on shore.

I've wandered through the jungles, contemplating God's singular goodness to me and knowing that I was perhaps the only person for a thousand miles in any direction that knew Him. Often, at such times, I would quote to myself the beautiful lines of Propertius:

> In desert wood, with Thee, my God,
> Where human footsteps never trod,
>     How happy could I be!
> Thou my repose from care, my Light,
> Amidst the darkness of the night,
>     In solitude my company.

During that second voyage, God wonderfully protected me from dangers I did not even know about at the time. Once, my crew plotted to capture the ship and turn pirate. Just as they were about to make their move—waiting only for the right time—two of the ringleaders fell ill. One died. That ended the affair for the moment and led to its discovery. The consequences would have been fatal for me if the Lord had not intervened.

The slaves on board were constantly plotting to revolt. Sometimes, they were on the brink of making their move, but I always found out about it in time to prevent them. When I have thought myself the safest, I have been suddenly alarmed with the danger. And when I have almost despaired of my life, God has given me a sudden deliverance.

One time I was at a place called Mana, near Cape Mount on the African shore. I had been conducting some large transactions and had business to settle on shore. I left the ship in the morning; but, when I came near the shore, the surf ran so high that I was almost afraid to land. I had gone on through at worse times than that, but I felt an inward pause that I could not account for. Using the surf as an excuse, I returned to the ship. I had never done that before in all the time I was engaged in trade.

I soon learned why that had happened. The day before I intended to land, some anonymous person had spread a scandalous and groundless rumor about me that would have threatened my honor and my business interests perhaps for the rest of my life, if I had landed as I planned. I was angry when I discovered what had happened, but the Lord comforted me. I heard no more about the accusation until the next voyage, when it was publicly called a malicious hoax without a grain of truth.

Such things did not occur every day, fortunately, and I was able to schedule my time to my best advantage. I allotted eight hours for sleep and meals, eight hours for exercise and spiritual devotions, and eight hours for study. I had picked up my Latin once more. By charting my hours, I was able to fill up the whole day and seldom found that I had time on my hands with nothing to do. My studies of the classics kept me busy, but they were hardly worth the time they took, because they prompted me to admire false models of manhood and false rules for life. I think I might have profited more if I had read Cassandra or Cleopatra than I got from reading Livy.

From the coast of Africa I went to Saint Christopher's in the West Indies, and there my foolishness was its own punishment. I did not know that the letters my wife had written me had been forwarded to Antigua because originally I was supposed to land there. She was always so punctual about writing me, so I just assumed when I did not hear from her at all that she was probably dead. The more I thought about this, the more convinced I became that it was true. I lost my appetite, and I could not sleep. I developed a constant pain in my stomach that became so bad in three weeks' time I thought I'd had a stroke. I was suffering from a broken heart.

My malady was not all grief, however. Conscience had a share. I thought God was punishing me for my unfaithfulness to Him, especially for my reluctance to speak to my wife of spiritual things. What stung me most was the thought that I had lost forever the opportunity to share my love and His love with her. I would have given the world to know she was living and that I would have another opportunity to make up to her for my past failures.

When I had suffered like that for several weeks, the thought occurred to me to send a small boat to Antigua. I did so, and it brought back several packages of letters from her. Those letters restored my peace of mind—and my health—at once. She was alive! How good the Lord was to me, and how wicked were my unbelief and ingratitude toward Him.

In August 1753, I returned to Liverpool. My stay at home was very short that voyage. I had only six weeks.

# Letter 13

## My Last Trip

My dear Haweis:

Before I sailed on my third trip, I met a young man who had been a shipmate of mine on board the *Harwich* when we were boys. He had been, at the time I first knew him, a very serious young man, and I had done my best to liven him up. I had been only too successful.

Meeting now at Liverpool, we took up where we left off. He had good sense, and he had read many good books. Our conversation frequently turned to religion, and I did my very best to bring him back to his senses—as far as God was concerned. I gave him my testimony as clearly as I could, telling him how I was saved and showing him why that was the reason for the great change in me. I used every argument I knew to bring him to conviction. When I bore down too hard, he would remind me that I was the one who started him on his notorious career in sin in the first place. I cannot tell you how often I sorrowed over this.

He had planned to go as a ship's master to Guinea. But before his ship was ready, his sponsor went into bankruptcy and his voyage was canceled. As he had no other job offers, I offered to take him with me as a companion so that he could get an idea of what the coast of Africa was like. My own sponsor was agreeable and said he would offer him a job when we got back.

My idea was not so much to give my friend knowledge of the business as to have more time to debate salvation with him. I was hoping that my arguments, my example, and my prayers might have some positive effect on him. I could not have been more mistaken, and I was given lots of time to regret my decision.

My friend swore like a trooper and had the kind of life that went with that habit. Day by day, he became worse. I saw in him a perfect example of what I had once been, and it was awkward for me to have a reminder of this always in front of me.

He not only turned a deaf ear to all my pleadings, but he did everything he could to counteract my influence with my crew. He was a high spirited man, and it required all my patience, wisdom, and authority to hold him in check. He was a sharp thorn in my side for quite a time.

Eventually, I had a chance of buying a small sailing ship and supplying it with a cargo of my own. I gave him the command and sent him on his way to trade, using my ship's account as his guarantee.

The day he left, I repeated my advice to him to turn to Christ. I believe his friendship and his respect for me were as fine as could be expected from a man whose principles were diametrically opposed to mine. He seemed quite impressed with what I was saying when he left, but actually my words had no influence on him. When he found himself free of me, he fed every appetite he had. His violent life, coupled with the heat of the climate, threw him into a malignant fever. He died within a few days, convinced that I was right, but spiritually unchanged.

The account of his death I got from those who were with him was very graphic. His rage and despair struck them all with horror. He told them he knew he was going to hell, but he died without giving any indication that he either hoped or asked for mercy.

I thought I would give you this story, Haweis, because it stands in such contrast to the remarkable goodness God has shown to me, the chief of sinners.

I left the coast in about four months and sailed for Saint Christopher's island. Before this, I'd had perfect health, no matter what climate I was in. But on this trip I caught a fever that almost did me in. I wrote some letters, spelling out in detail what I went through at this time. When I wrote one of them, I could hardly hold a pen and thought I might never be able to write again.

Spiritually, I realized that I had no assurance that I would be with Christ if I died. But my hopes were greater than my fears, and I had a rest of heart that enabled me to wait for death without any panic. My trust, though weak, was fixed on the blood and righteousness of the Lord Jesus. The words "He is able also to save them to the uttermost" (Hebrews 7:25) really eased my mind. For a while I was bothered by one thought—whether it was a temptation or whether the fever twisted my mind, I don't know—but I was less afraid of God's wrath and punishment than I was of being lost and overlooked among the millions of souls who were continually entering the unseen world.

*What is my soul,* I thought, *among such an uncountable multitude?* I was afraid the Lord wouldn't notice me. I was all confused about this for quite some time, until I thought of a verse that put it out of my mind: "The Lord knoweth them that are his" (2 Timothy 2:19).

In about ten days, even though my crew thought I was dying, I began to get well. In fact, by the time we arrived in the West Indies, I was completely recovered.

Now for about six years the Lord had been leading me secretly in His path. I had learned something of the evil of my own heart, and I had read the Bible and several other good books over and over again. I had a general view of gospel truths, but I did not have a clear idea of biblical principles. One reason, I felt, was that I had never met anyone who could answer my questions.

But when I arrived at Saint Christopher's this time, I found a captain of a ship from London who was really able to help me. He was a mature Christian and a lively conversationalist. We discovered each other by accident one evening as we chatted at a gathering of mutual friends; and we soon became, as much as our business would allow, inseparable. For nearly a month we spent every evening together on board each other's ship alternately. And often we talked through the night. I simply could not learn enough.

He not only taught my mind, but he taught my heart. He encouraged me to open my mouth more in public prayer. He said I could learn much from talking more openly with Christian people. He urged me to testify in public and to speak to people about the Lord more freely.

The Lord used him to clear up my misconceptions about biblical things. I became more evangelical, and I was delivered from the fear of falling into my former way of life. I now began to understand the security of the believer in the covenant of grace. And I learned that I could not keep myself from sin by my own power and holiness but by trusting the mighty power and promise of God through faith in my unchangeable Savior.

My friend informed me of the religious errors and controversies of the times, things I had never heard of before. And he told me where to go in London to find others who could teach me. I left Saint Christopher's far richer than I had come, and my trip home gave me plenty of time to digest what I had received. It was an uneventful trip, so I had lots of time to think and study. I arrived in Liverpool in August 1754.

By the beginning of November I was ready again to go to sea, but the Lord had other plans.

During the time I was busy in the slave trade, I never had one doubt as to its lawfulness. I was satisfied that it was God's provision for me to earn my way. It was the kind of thing a gentleman would do, and usually it was very profitable—though I didn't find it particularly so. The Lord must have felt that great wealth would not be good for me.

I considered myself a jailer, but sometimes it bothered me that my time was constantly spent chaining, bolting, and shackling people. I had often prayed that the Lord in His own time would give me another vocation—a more humane one—in which I could have more frequent fellowship with His people and His service. I longed to be freed from the long separations from home. That was the hardest part of my life.

My prayers were answered, though not in the way I expected.

I was within two days of sailing and seemed in good health. But in the afternoon, as I was sitting with my wife, drinking tea and talking over the recent weeks we had shared together, I was knocked senseless by some kind of seizure.

It lasted about an hour; but, when I recovered, the pain and dizziness in my head convinced the doctors that it would be foolish for me to go to sea just then. I consulted with my friend who owned the ship, and he convinced me that I should stay home. I resigned the command the day before she sailed. In this way I was unexpectedly freed from that vocation and, fortunately for me, from the consequences of that particular trip. My replacement died, along with most of the officers and many of the crew, and the vessel was brought back home with great difficulty.

Now that I was relieved of that business I left Liverpool and spent most of the following year in London and Kent. But I had a new trial. The blow that knocked me senseless affected my wife as well. We didn't realize it at first, because she herself didn't feel it. But as I grew better and her fear for me subsided, we found out what a shock it had been to her system. The doctors could not diagnose what was wrong, and they could not give her any medicines to cure it. She had none of the symptoms of tuberculosis, but her health broke down right before our eyes. She became so weak she could hardly bear anyone to walk across the room she was in. For eleven months I sat beside her. Dr. Young called my new employment the "dreadful post of observation, darker every hour."

But after we settled down at Liverpool, the Lord restored my wife to her former health, when we had all but given up hope.

# Letter 14

## My Life at Home

My dear Haweis:

Using the directions I had received from my captain friend at Saint Christopher's, I found Christian friends in London. I went to Mr. Brewer's church and received real help from his public and private ministry to me. He became a wonderful friend of mine; of all my friends he was perhaps the closest. I had another choice friend who was really excited about the Lord's service. We wrote one another frequently until his final illness.

When Mr. Whitefield returned from America, my two good friends introduced me to him. I didn't get to know him personally until later, but I found his ministry a real help to me just then. I fellowshiped with several Christian groups and met many excellent men and women of God. So, when I was in London, I felt I was at the source of spiritual ministry. But when I was in Kent, it was far different. Although I did find some very serious people there, the chief advantage to me was the woodland countryside. I spent several hours every day, when the weather was fair, in the thickest woods and on the highest hills, where almost every step presented new views to me.

I love having my devotions outside, and these country places refreshed and calmed my spirit. When I get away from the hubbub of modern life, I think of myself as in the great temple that the Lord has built for His own honor.

I used to wander through the country between Rochdale and Maidstone, bordering on the Medway; and if I could take you there now, I could show you many places where I earnestly sought and happily found the Lord's comfortable presence with my soul.

All this time, of course, I was deeply concerned about my wife's illness. She grew worse, and we began to fear for her life. In faith, I gave her to the Lord. She was His to do with as He pleased. But too often, my heart rebelled, and I found it hard to either trust or submit to Him.

I was also concerned about my future. There was a glut of slaves on the market that year, and my friends did not want to outfit another ship until mine returned. So I was in suspense about how I would support my family.

In August I received word that I had been appointed to the office of tide surveyor. Such jobs do not come easily. Normally they go only to those who work hard to get them. But it came to me without my seeking or expecting it. I knew my good friends in Liverpool had tried to have me appointed to another post, but they found it had gone to someone else. I later learned that job would not have interested me in the slightest. This one was the very thing I would have wanted. It gave me a great deal of free time and the liberty of living my own way, while earning my keep. The good hand of the Lord was in it, I knew.

But getting the appointment only doubled my anxiety for my wife. The job required that I leave her for some weeks, and she was suffering great pain and sickness. The physicians didn't know what to do, and I had no hope that I would ever see her alive again. I had to go, but I could not leave. I could only trust my Father. And, you know, He gave me real peace and strength. He took the matter completely out of my mind until the day before I was to go. He even gave me the strength to commit both her and myself to His perfect will; so, for some reason, I was able to leave her cheerfully.

Soon after I left, she began to recover. In fact, she came around so fast I was able to meet her at Stone, fully recovered, two months later when she came to me at Liverpool.

Since October 1755, we have been living comfortably here in Liverpool. Even though our trials have been light and few, we have remembered every day that our lives must be lives of faith. My chief trial is the body of sin and death that makes me sigh, as Paul did, "O wretched man that I am! who shall deliver me from the body of this death?" And then with him I can say, "I thank God through Jesus Christ our Lord" (Romans 7:24-25).

I live in a country where both the knowledge of God and the power of God are little known. But living here has given me time to soak up the spiritual truths I heard when I was in London. I had many notions that could not be backed up with Scripture, but my faithful Teacher ministered His truth to me through His Word and experience. My slow, deliberate study helped me to solidify the things I had learned superficially before.

I admit that at times I have gone to extremes when I should be living in the golden center of His will, but the Lord has helped me to profit from my mistakes. I am still a learner, and I have learned very little, but I am trusting Him to carry on His work in my soul and graciously to increase my knowledge of Him and of myself.

Since my business gave me so much time to study and since I decided I would "know nothing but Jesus Christ and Him crucified," I put every thought of the classics and mathematics out of my head and began to study Greek. I wanted to learn enough to be able to understand both the New Testament and the Septuagint. The next year I took up Hebrew, and two years after that, Syriac, since I saw it would be to my advantage to be able to read it, too.

Oh, I have no unusual skill in any one of these—I will never be a scholar. But I wanted to be able to learn the significance of scriptural words and phrases. In Hebrew, I can read the historical books of the Old Testament and Psalms easily enough. In the prophets I have to use the lexicons to look up words. But I am able, using these helps, to figure out the meaning of any passage I want. More than that I do not want. I would rather help people than die with the reputation of having been an eminent linguist.

I have also studied some of the best commentaries in English, Latin, and French. More recently, however, I have begun to write and have not had time for more than the Scriptures themselves.

In all my literary attempts, I have had to strike out on my own, since I have not had a teacher since I was ten years old.

I have told you, Haweis, that Mother hoped that I would enter the ministry. Her death and the kind of life I lived after that seemed to end that likelihood. But the desire to do this began to grow in my mind as I was meditating on Paul's statement in Galatians 1:23-24: "But they had heard only, that he which persecuted us in times past now preacheth the faith which once he destroyed. And they glorified God in me."

I wanted to tell others of God's divine grace; I thought I was—perhaps above most others—just the person to proclaim that "Christ Jesus came into the world to save sinners; of whom I am chief" (1 Timothy 1:15). Since my life had been full of unbelievable twists and turns, I was hoping that sooner or later God might call me into His service.

It was partly with that in mind that I studied Greek and Hebrew Scriptures, but I really didn't do anything about it until some Christian friends encouraged me to. At first, I questioned the idea;

but after thinking about it for some time, praying about it, and talking to my friends, I became convinced that that was what I should do.

My first thought was to join the Dissenters. Since 1757 I'd had a lot to do with believers in West Riding, a part of Yorkshire. The gospel was flourishing there, and I had learned much from the ministry of the Word and from the Lord's people.

Since I still preferred the Established Church in some ways, I asked the Archbishop of York for ordination. I do not need to tell you that he refused. At present (1763), I still want to serve the Lord. But I am not pushing myself forward, as I did at first. It is sufficient that the Lord knows how to use me. He can and will do what is best. I am His to use. I want His will and my best interests to be one and the same. To His Name be glory.

# Epilogue

## A Further Account of John Newton's Life

## Abridged from the Work of the Reverend R. Cecil

On December 16, 1758, John Newton applied to the Archbishop of York for ordination. The Bishop of Chester countersigned his references and referred John to a Dr. Newton, the archbishop's chaplain. He was then referred to the archbishop's secretary, who informed him that he had "represented the matter to the archbishop, but His Grace was inflexible in supporting the rules and canons of the Church."

John had done a little preaching in Liverpool, and many who heard him encouraged him to speak more widely. He wrote to his wife: "The death of the late Reverend Mr. Jones of Saint Saviour's Church has impressed me more about my entering the ministry. It would be wrong, after having so seriously devoted myself to the Lord for His service, to waste my time and bury my talents in silence, just because I have been refused ordination in the Established Church. The Lord has done great things for me!

"The way I feel at this point is not something only I am feeling. I have known several men—sensible, godly, and competent members in good standing of the Established Church—who, tired of being refused time after time when they applied for ordination, have struck off into an itinerant ministry or have settled among the Dissenters. Some of these men are still living and are useful in their ministry."

In 1764 John was recommended by Lord Dartmouth to Dr. Green, Bishop of Lincoln, to fill the pulpit of Olney. He was ordained and installed. He found many people in the congregation had evangelical views of the truth and were mature in the light and experience of it. The vicarage was the gift of the Earl of Dartmouth, the nobleman to whom John had addressed the first twenty-six letters in his book *Cardiphonia*. The earl was a godly man and a kind one. He had previously appointed a Reverend Moses Brown the vicar of Olney. Brown was an evangelical minister and a good man who ably taught the believers there. He had also led many of them to Christ.

John stayed at Olney nearly sixteen years. While there, the Lord used him to help relieve the depressed mind of the poet William Cowper. He also lived near the Reverend Thomas Scott, then pastor of Ravenstone and Weston Underwood churches, a man whose ministry and writings have been so helpful to mankind.

In the year 1776, John was afflicted with a tumor on his thigh. As it grew larger and more troublesome, he underwent surgery in London. He was more concerned that he demonstrate the patience of a Christian in pain than that he find relief.

"I felt," he said, "that being able to bear a very sharp operation with calmness and confidence was a greater favor granted by God to me than getting rid of my malady."

In October 1777, a terrible fire broke out in the town of Olney, and John took an active part in comforting and collecting money for those who suffered.

Although we have no actual instance of Newton's suffering persecution for his ministry at Olney, we do know that "all that will live godly in Christ Jesus shall suffer persecution" (2 Timothy 3:12). I have heard him say, "When God is about to do any great work, He generally allows some great opposition to emerge. Suppose Pharaoh had immediately consented to the departure of the children of Israel, or suppose that the children of Israel had met with no difficulties on their way to the Promised Land, passing from Egypt into Canaan with ease. They—and the church in all future ages —would have been great losers. They would never have seen the wonder-working God deliver them from their adversaries and trials. A smooth passage for them would have made a poor story for us."

John's ministry at Olney was characterized by the verse "The servant of the Lord must not strive; but be gentle unto all men, apt to teach, patient." To the last day he spent among those people, Newton continued "in meekness instructing those that [opposed], if God peradventure [might] give them repentance to the acknowledging of the truth" (2 Timothy 2:24-25).

During this time he published several books. One volume, *Sermons*, is marked, "Liverpool, January 1, 1760." In 1762 he published his *Omicron*, to which his letters, signed "Vigil," were later added. In 1764 his *Narrative* appeared; in 1767, a volume of sermons preached at Olney. In 1769, his *Review of Ecclesiastical History* was published, and in 1770, a volume of hymns (some of which were composed by William Cowper and prefixed with a "C" to distinguish them from the ones John wrote). In 1781 he published his valuable work *Cardiphonia*.

From Olney, John was appointed to the united parishes of Saint Mary, Woolnoth, and Saint Mary, Woolchurch Haw, Lombard-Street, London, on the "presentation" of his friend Mr. John Thornton. Some difficulty came up concerning Mr. Thornton's right to appoint, that right being claimed by a nobleman. The question was eventually brought before the House of Lords and settled in favor of Mr. Thornton. John preached his first sermon to his congregations on December 19, 1779 from Ephesians 4:15, on "speaking the truth in love." A message of comfort and love, that sermon was immediately published in tract form.

Placed in the center of London in a wealthy neighborhood, John had a course of service that was in several ways different from his former position at Olney. But being a man of the Book and a student of the heart of man, he proposed no other weapons for pulling down the strongholds of sin and Satan around him than the Word of God.

He was constantly astonished at the grace of God in rescuing him from his former life and putting him in the ministry in London.

He said on many occasions, "That one of the most ignorant, the most miserable, and the most abandoned of slaves should be plucked from his forlorn state of exile on the coast of Africa and eventually be appointed minister of the parish of the first magistrate of the first city in the world; that he should there not only testify to such grace, but himself be a monument of it; that he should be able to record his rescue in his history, preaching, and writings to the world at large is a fact that I marvel in but could never sufficiently understand."

He always showed himself as a friendly, likable man. His home was open to Christians of all ranks and denominations. Here, like a father among his children, he used to entertain, encourage, and instruct his friends—especially younger ministers or candidates for the ministry. Here also the poor, the sick, and the tempted found a refuge and sympathy they could scarcely find to the same degree anywhere else.

John's timely hints on Christian living and on truth were to the point, and they profited his listeners much. Some time after he published his book *Omicron*, in which he described three stages of Christian growth—first the blade, then the ear, and then the full corn in the ear (he distinguished them by the letters A, B, and C)—he received a letter from a young minister, who wrote telling that Newton had accurately described his character. The young man said he was a "C."

Newton wrote back that when he had described the character of "C" as full maturity he had forgotten to add that a "C" never knew his own face. A person who is mature never takes pride in his own maturity.

On another occasion John said, "It grieves me to see so few of my wealthy parishioners coming to church. The rich are under a greater obligation to hear the preaching of the gospel than the poor. For at church, the rich must hear the whole truth as well as others. They have no escape. But let them once get home, and you'll have a time getting at them. When you are admitted, you are so shackled with 'punctilio,' so interrupted and drowned with the foolish conversation of their friends that, as Archbishop Leighton says, 'It is well if your visit does not prove a blank or a blot.' "

He would use every opportunity he could to teach lessons to his flock. One night he found a notice put up at Saint Mary, Woolnoth, on which he commented a great deal when he got up to preach.

The notice read: "A young man, having come to the possession of a very large fortune, desires the prayers of the congregation that he may be preserved from the snares to which it exposes him."

"Now, if that man," Newton said, "had *lost* a fortune, the world would not have wondered to have seen him put up such a notice. But this man has been better taught."

Coming out of church on a Wednesday night, he was stopped by a lady who said, "The ticket in which I hold a quarter interest has drawn a prize of $50,000. I know you will congratulate me on this occasion."

"Madam," he said, "as for a friend under temptation, I will endeavor to pray for you."

One day he expressed his grief that a minister he knew was paying too much attention to politics.

"For my part," he said, "I have no temptation to turn politician, and much less to inflame anyone in these times. When a ship is leaky and a spirit of mutiny divides the crew, a wise man would say, 'My good friends, while we are debating, the water is gaining on us. We had better leave the debate and go to the pumps.'

"I want to turn peoples' eyes from men to God. I am continually attempting to show them how far they are from knowing either the facts of a given case or the rights. I want people to appreciate the great privileges we have in this country, and I advise the discontented to go live a little while in Russia."

He said of the continual interruptions he faced, "I see in this world two heaps of human happiness and misery. If I can take the smallest bit from one heap and add it to the other, I do a service. If, as I go home, I pass a child who has lost a penny, and —by giving him another—I can wipe away his tears, I feel I have done something worthwhile. I would be glad to do greater things, but I will not neglect little things like that. When I hear a knock on my study door, I hear a message from God. It may be a lesson of instruction or a lesson of patience. But since it is His message, it must be interesting."

John used to spend a month or two annually at the house of some friend in the country. He always said good-bye to his congregation affectionately before he left and spoke of his return as uncertain, since any number of events could prevent it. Everyone was impressed that he considered the hand of God in every event, no matter how trivial it might look to others. On every occasion, in the business of every hour, in matters public or private, like Enoch he "walked with God."

John experienced a great shock soon after he came to Saint Mary's, when his fourteen-year-old niece, Eliza Cunningham, died. She was a lovely girl, and he loved her as if she were his own. She had not only a friendly nature, but a real godliness. Mr. and Mrs. Newton watched her gradually sink into death. Fully prepared to meet her heavenly Father, she died October 6, 1785.

But a still greater loss was to follow. He had always loved his wife dearly. In fact he once confessed to a group of friends that while he was courting her he took many trips out of London to Shooter's Hill in Blackheath, just so he could look toward her house.

"I could not see the spot itself, for she lived far

beyond what I could see from the hill. But it satisfied me just to look toward the spot. I did this once —sometimes twice—a week."

How keenly he felt about her is clear in an excerpt from his book *Letters to a Wife*:

My dear wife had a naturally strong body and a cheerful personality. But the illness she had after my seizure weakened her. She suffered from time to time from an assortment of sicknesses. I believe she spent ten of the forty years we lived together in illness. But she did have long periods of good health.

Before we left Liverpool, she received a blow upon her left breast. This caused her some pain and anxiety for a little while, but it soon wore off. A small lump remained, but she made no mention of any discomfort for many years. Her love for me made her conceal it as long as she could. I have wondered since how she could keep so quiet about it, and why I was not more perceptive.

In October 1788, she went without my knowing about it to a mutual friend, an eminent surgeon. Her plan was, if he approved it, to submit to an operation that would be performed in my absence and before I could know about it. But the doctor told her that the sickness was too far advanced for surgery. The tumor, the size of half a melon, was too large to be removed without endangering her life. He could give her little advice, except to keep herself as quiet and her mind as easy as possible. He prescribed laudanum to ease the pain, but she disliked it so much that she hated to take it.

I cannot tell you how composed and resigned she was the next day when she told me what the surgeon had said. Nor can I tell you what went through

111

my mind and heart when I heard it. My conscience told me I deserved to be wounded where I was most sensitive and that it was my duty to submit to the will of the Lord in silence. I knew that, unless He gave me that kind of submission to His will, I was likely to toss like a wild bull in a net in defiance of my better judgment.

Soon after, the Lord let our dear adopted daughter, Elizabeth Catlett, suffer a dreadful fever. She nearly died, and we once or twice thought that she indeed had. But the Lord restored her and she's still living, the chief comfort to me in my old age.

That heavy trial lasted during the whole of a very severe winter. And it was very difficult for my wife to have the tranquil mind my surgeon friend told her she must preserve. She was often very tired and much alarmed. Next to each other, this dear child had the nearest place both in her heart and mine. The effects of the strain were soon apparent. As the spring of 1789 approached, her malady rapidly increased. Her pains were almost incessant and often intense. She could seldom lie one hour in bed in the same position. O my heart, what didst thou suffer!

But in April God mercifully gave her relief. Her illness went into remission, and her pains ended. Though I believe she never had an hour of perfect ease, she felt little of the distressing pains that were part of her malady from then until near the end of her life.

At the end of the summer she was able to go to Southampton. She returned tolerably well and was able to be in church twice the first week after she came home. Then she didn't go out anymore except to take a ride in a coach for a little air and exercise. She was cheerful and comfortable, and she slept as well as most people who are in perfect health. She was able to have friends come in, and she enjoyed their company.

I learned during this time to pity those who are ill and who do not have the comforts we had. Our distress was not small, but we had everything within reach that could in any way refresh or relieve my wife. We had faithful and affectionate servants who were always willing to attend and assist her by night or by day. What must it be like for those who, when they suffer awful diseases, pine away unpitied, unnoticed, without help, and without even the most ordinary necessities? I realized as never before that I had much more cause to be thankful rather than complaining.

For about a year her spirits were good, and her patience was an example to us all. She was cheerful in disposition and sweet in all her talk. Often her lively conversation would force a smile out of us, even though we had tears of love and pity in our eyes.

But whatever little occupation she had for her hands during the day she would do nothing until she had finished reading that day's Scripture portion. I have her Bible, in which almost every major text from beginning to end is marked in the margin with a pencil in her own handwriting. The good Word of God was her medicine and her food while she was able to read it. She also read Dr. Watt's *Psalms* and *Hymns* and the *Olney Hymns* in the same manner. There are few of them in which one, two, or more verses are not marked. In many—those I suppose she read more frequently —every verse is marked.

Then one other thing happened that made matters worse. It had been her custom when she went from her sofa to her bed to show me how well she could walk. She did this to encourage me, I'm sure. But the Lord allowed some dislocation to affect her spine, so that she couldn't move herself, and it was extremely difficult for any of the rest of us to move her. It has taken five of us nearly two hours to move her from one side of the bed to the other. At times, even this was not practical, and she had to lie in one spot for more than a week.

I wondered if all this was necessary on my account—whether the Lord let this happen to her so He could reach me. The rod had a voice, and it was the voice of the Lord. I understood the meaning as if He had spoken it audibly from heaven and said, "Now contemplate this one you've idolized. Now see what *she* is, whom you once presumed to prefer to *Me!*" But I knew the Lord is not vindictive.

He gave her sweetness and patience. When I would say, "You suffer greatly," she would answer, "I do suffer, but not greatly." And she often expressed her thankfulness that, though she couldn't move her body, she was still able to use her hands.

One of the last concerns she felt in this world was when my close friend and benefactor, John Thornton, died. She revered him more than any person on earth, and she had reason. Few were closer to him than we and few were under greater obligation to him than we. She had known he was ill, but I had kept the progress of his illness from her. I hadn't wanted to upset her further, and she was afraid to ask.

I had to tell her where I was going when I left for his funeral. I would be gone four or five hours, and I hardly expected to find her alive at my return.

114

She eagerly replied, 'Go, by all means. I would not have you stay with me upon any consideration.'

I put the funeral ring they gave me into her hands when I got back. She put it first to her lips and then to her eyes as she wept. She survived him more than a month.

Her head bore the brunt of her illness. She could not bear the sound of the gentlest foot on the carpet, nor the softest voice. I could do little more than sit and look at her. On Sunday, December 12, as I was preparing for church in the morning, she sent for me, and we said a final farewell. She faintly spoke one of her sweet names for me and gave me her hand which I held as I prayed for her by her bedside. We exchanged a few tears, but I was as unable to speak as she was.

I returned soon after and said, "If your mind is in a state of peace, it will comfort me if you can signify it by holding up your hand." She held it up and waved it to and fro several times.

That evening her speech, her sight, and—I believe —her hearing wholly failed. She lay there quietly without showing any sign of pain or uneasiness until Wednesday evening toward seven o'clock. Then she began to breathe very hard. Her breathing might be called groaning, for they could hear it in every part of the house. But she lay quite still with a placid expression on her face, as if she were in a gentle sleep. There was no start or struggle, and not a feature winced.

I took my post beside her bed and watched her for nearly three hours. I sat there with a candle in my hand until I saw her breathe her last a little before ten in the evening, December 15, 1790. When I was sure she was gone, I took off her ring, as she had instructed me, and put it on my own finger. Then I kneeled down with the servants who were in the room and thanked the Lord for delivering her from her pain and for her peaceful entrance into His presence.

About two or three months before her death when I was walking up and down the room, offering disjointed prayers, a thought suddenly struck me with unusual force. *Grief is self-indulgence. The Lord wants us to be at peace. We should resist grief with all our strength.* I instantly said aloud, "Lord, I am helpless, indeed, in myself, but I hope I am willing without any reservation for You to help me." And since the promises of God are true, I knew the Lord would be willing to help me if I was willing to be helped.

All the time my dear wife was down, I kept mulling over this matter of grief. I was a minister, and many people were watching to see how I would react to her affliction. I had told people whom I comforted that the gospel is an effective remedy for every evil and a full provision for everyone in need. Afflicted believers will only be unhappy when they indulge in self-will and unbelief. I often told my listeners that trials for a Christian were a badge of honor, giving us the opportunity to show others that we walk in the good of God's grace.

I prayed daily that I wouldn't by some act of impatience or anxiety contradict my teaching. I wanted to practice what I preached. I didn't want someone to come to me with the words Eliphaz said to Job: "Thy words have upholden him that was falling, and thou hast strengthened the feeble knees [of others]. But now it is come upon thee, and thou faintest; it toucheth thee, and thou art troubled" (Job 4:4-5).

It was good I prayed. From the time I told my

Father that I was willing to be helped, my heart did trust in Him and He really helped me. Through the whole period of Mary's illness, I preached at every service and performed all my pastoral duties. A stranger wouldn't have discovered either by my words or my looks that my wife was so troubled. Many of our intimate friends feared that her long illness and especially her death would overwhelm me. But that was not the case. I even preached on the day of her death.

After she was gone, I'm sure I broke some of the rules of etiquette that insist a mourner mourn. Some people notice this more than they do outright sin. But I didn't want to sit at home and pore over my loss. I went out and visited some of my friends the very next day. I preached three times while she lay dead.

Some of my friends offered to take over my preaching for this time, but since the Lord was giving me strength in body and mind, I felt it was my duty to conduct all my services. After she was buried, I preached her funeral sermon with little more emotion than if it had been for another person. I hope many of my hearers were comforted in their own affliction by what they saw of the Lord's goodness to me. It was worth going through that fire, so that I might show the good of God's power and faithfulness.

His Word also brought me comfort. I saw again what I had seen before, but now I saw it more clearly: I, as a sinner, had no *rights*, and I, as a believer, could have no *reason* to complain. He had loaned her to me, and He who loaned her had a right to take her back when He chose. Had He given me what I deserved, He would have taken her back the first day I got her. I was just thankful I'd had her so long.

His sovereignty is connected to His infinite wisdom and goodness. If it were possible for me to alter any part of His plan, I could only spoil it. I'm such a short-sighted person—so blind to the possible consequences of my own wishes. I'm not only unworthy; I'm not even able to choose well for myself. So it was certainly to my great benefit that the Lord condescended to choose for me.

In that same year a university in New Jersey conferred an honorary Doctor of Divinity degree upon John and sent him the diploma. He also received a work in two volumes that had been dedicated to him. The letters *D.D.* were added to his name. He wrote back that he was grateful for the gift, but he asked to decline the honor as one he never intended to accept.

"I am," he said, "as one born out of due time. I don't wish to have honors of this kind. No matter how much the university overrates my accomplishments, and no matter how it wishes to show its respects, I must not forget who I am. It would be conceited and improper for me to allow it."

Newton regularly made trips in the summer to visit different friends in the country, and he tried to make the visits profitable to them and their neighbors by holding little Bible studies morning and evening. Some were brought to a saving knowledge of Christ by attending. He seldom entered a room without communicating something both profitable and entertaining.

His friends were delighted and surprised that he should grow old so gracefully. Though almost eighty years old, his sight nearly gone, and nearly deaf, he continued his public ministry with a great deal of his former liveliness. His memory failed, but his judgment in spiritual things still remained. He used to account for his occasional depression by saying it was because he was getting old. But his perception was clear, and his zeal for the truths he had taught for so long was unflagging. Like Simeon, having seen the salvation of the Lord, he now only waited and prayed to depart in peace.

After he turned eighty, some of his friends were concerned that he not extend his public ministry too long. He was less able to expound the Scriptures in the pulpit, and he had lost his strength. Although he was occasionally depressed, he testified that he still held tenaciously to the principles God had taught him.

Someone asked, "In the matter of public preaching, might it not be best to consider your work as done and stop before you discover you can no longer speak?"

He answered, raising his voice, "I cannot stop. What? Shall the old African blasphemer stop while he can speak?" His last sermon was preached in October 1806, for a fund to aid widows and orphans of Trafalgar.

As Newton's health began to decline, his friends found that he occasionally didn't recognize them. His sight, hearing, and memory failed; but not having much pain, he generally appeared easy and cheerful. And he didn't deny his faith in all his weakness. He held to the truth through it all.

His strength gradually failed until it was painful for anyone to ask him a question or attempt to rouse the old faculties that were once so bright.

People wonder how he left this world. He used to say, "Tell me not how a man died, but how he lived."

About a month before his death, John said, "It is a great thing to die and, when flesh and heart fail, to have God for the strength of our heart and our portion forever. I know whom I have believed and am persuaded that He is able to keep that which I have committed unto Him against that day. Henceforth there is laid up for me a crown of righteousness which the Lord, the righteous Judge, shall give me at that day."

Later to his niece, he said, "I have been meditating on a subject, 'Come, and hear, all ye that fear God, and I will declare what He hath done for my soul.'"

At another time he said, "More light, more love, more liberty. Hereafter I hope, when I shut my eyes on the things of time I shall open them in a better world. What a thing it is to live under the shadow of the wings of the Almighty! I am going the way of all flesh."

And when one replied, "The Lord is gracious," he answered, "If it were not so, how could I dare to stand before Him?"

The Wednesday before he died, when asked if his mind was comfortable, he replied, "I am satisfied with the Lord's will."

John seemed sensible to his last hour. He died December 21, 1807, and was buried in the vault of his church ten days later.

He left these instructions for the executors of his estate:

"I propose writing an epitaph for myself, if it may be put up on a plain marble tablet near the vestry door, to the following purport:

JOHN NEWTON, Clerk,
Once an infidel and libertine,
A servant of slaves in Africa,
Was, by the rich mercy of our Lord and Saviour,
JESUS CHRIST,
Preserved, restored, pardoned,
And appointed to preach the faith
He had long laboured to destroy,
Near sixteen years at Olney, in Bucks,
And _____ years in this church.
On February 1, 1750, he married
MARY,
Daughter of the late George Catlett,
of Chatham, Kent.
He resigned her to the Lord who gave her,
On the 15th day of December, 1790.

And I earnestly desire that no monument and no inscription but to this purport may be attempted for me."

The following is a copy of the beginning of his will, dated June 13, 1803:

In the name of God, Amen. I, John Newton, of Coleman Street Buildings, in the parish of Saint Stephen, Coleman Street, in the city of London, clerk, being through mercy in good health and of sound and disposing mind, memory, and understanding, although in the seventy-eighth year of my age, do for the settling of my temporal concerns and for the disposal of all the worldly estate which it hath pleased the Lord in His good providence to give me, make this my last will and testament as follows:

I commit my soul to my gracious God and Savior, who mercifully spared and preserved me, when I was an apostate, a blasphemer, and an infidel, and delivered me from that state of misery on the coast of Africa into which my obstinate wickedness had plunged me; and who has been pleased to admit me, though most unworthy, to preach His glorious gospel. I rely with humble confidence upon the atonement and mediation of the Lord Jesus Christ, God and Man, which I have often proposed to others, as the only foundation whereupon a sinner can build his hope, trusting that He will guard and guide me through the uncertain remainder of my life, and that He will then admit me into His presence in His heavenly kingdom.

I would have my body deposited in the vault under the parish church of Saint Mary, Woolnoth —close to the coffins of my late dear wife and my dear niece Elizabeth Cunningham—and it is my desire that my funeral may be performed with as little expense as possible, consistent with decency.

# Appendix

## Some Remarks Made by John Newton in Familiar Conversation

"When a Christian goes into the world because he sees it as his *call*, as long as he also sees it as his *cross*, it will not hurt him. Satan will seldom come to a Christian with a gross temptation; a green log and a candle may be safely left together. But bring a few shavings, then some small sticks, and then larger ones, and you will soon make ashes of that green log."

"If two angels were sent from Heaven to execute a divine command—one to conduct an empire and the other to sweep a street in it—they would feel no inclination to change employments."

"What some call providential openings are often powerful temptations. The heart, when wandering, cries, 'Here is a way opened before me.' But the way that looks providential should be rejected, perhaps, and not walked."

"A Christian should never say the reason he is sloppy is because he is spiritual. If he is only a shoe shiner, he should be the best in the parish."

"My principal method of defeating heresy is by establishing truth. If someone wants to fill a bushel with tares, I can defy his attempts by first filling it with wheat."

"Many have puzzled about the origin of evil. I observe there is evil and there is a way to escape it, and with this I begin and end."

"Consecrated things under the law were first sprinkled with blood, and then anointed with oil. After that they were no longer common. Thus, under the gospel, every Christian has been a common vessel for profane purposes; but when sprinkled and anointed, he becomes separated and consecrated to God."

"A Christian in the world is like a man who has had a long intimacy with one whom he eventually finds has been the murderer of his kind father. The intimacy after this will surely be broken."

"Honesty will always allow much for inexperience. I have been thirty years forming my own views, and in the course of this time some of my hills have been sinking and some of my valleys have risen. But how unreasonable it would be to expect that all this should take place in another person in the course of a year or two."

"I can imagine that a man can live without an arm or leg, but not without a head or heart. So there are some truths that are essential to vital religion—truths all awakened souls should be taught."

"A Christian is like a young nobleman who, on going to receive his estate, is at first enchanted with his prospects. This in course of time may wear off, but his sense of the value of the estate grows daily."

"When we first enter into the Christian life, we expect to grow rich. God's plan is to make us feel poor."

"Once when I was going to take a new pastorate, I was reading as I walked in a green lane, 'Fear not, Paul, I have much people in this city.' Soon afterwards, I was disappointed to find that Paul was not John and that Corinth was not Warwick."

"Christ has taken our nature into Heaven to represent us and has left us on earth with His nature to represent Him."

"Worldly men will be true to their principles. If we were as true to ours as they are to theirs, the visits between the parties would be short and seldom."

"A Christian in the world is like a man transacting his affairs in the rain. He will not suddenly leave his client because it rains. But the moment the business is done, he is off. As it is said in the book of Acts, 'Being let go, they went to their own company.'"

"God deals with us as we do with our children. He first speaks, then gives a gentle stroke, and at last a blow."

"The religion of a sinner stands on two pillars: namely, what Christ did for him in His flesh and what He performs in him by His Spirit. Most errors arise from an attempt to separate these two."

"The word 'temperance' in the New Testament signifies self-possession. It is the frame of mind of a person with a race to run and who therefore does not load his pockets with lead."

"Take a toy away from a child and give him another, and he is satisfied. But if he is hungry, no toy will do. Thus as newborn babes, true believers desire the sincere milk of the Word. The desire for grace is, in this way, grace."

"One said that the great saints in the calendar

were, many of them, poor sinners. Mrs. Newton replied, 'They were poor saints, indeed, if they did not feel that they were great sinners.' "

"The Lord has reasons far beyond our understanding for opening a wide door while stopping the mouth of a useful preacher. John Bunyan would not have done half the good he did if he had remained preaching in Bedford instead of being shut up in Bedford prison."

"Professors who own the doctrines of free grace often act inconsistently with their own principles when they are angry at the defects in the lives of others. A company of travelers fall into a pit and one of them gets a passer-by to draw him out. Now he should not be angry with the rest for falling in, nor should he be angry that they are not yet out as he is for he did not pull himself out. Therefore, instead of scolding them, he should show them pity. He should not go down into the pit again but show how much better able he is to help them now that he is out of it. We should take care that we do not make our profession of religion an opportunity for us to cancel out all other obligations. A man truly illuminated will no more despise others than Bartimaeus, after his own eyes were opened, would take a stick and beat every blind man he met."

"It is pure mercy that says no to a particular request. A miser would pray very earnestly for gold if he believed prayer would gain it. But if Christ wanted to do him a favor, He would take his gold away. A child walks in the garden in spring and sees cherries. He knows they are good fruit and asks for them. 'No, dear,' says the father, 'they are not yet ripe. Wait until they are ripe.' "

"If I cannot take pleasure in infirmities, I can sometimes feel the profit of them. I can conceive that a king can pardon a rebel and take him into his family and say, 'I appoint you for a season to wear a chain. At a certain season I will send a messenger to knock it off. In the meantime this chain will remind you of your state. Perhaps it will humble you and restrain you from wandering.' "

"I have read of many wicked popes, but the worst pope I have ever met is Pope Self."

"The heir of a great estate, while a child, thinks more of a few cents in his pocket than of his inheritance. So a Christian is often happier by some frame of heart than he is by his title to glory."

"I feel like a man who has no money in his pocket, but is allowed to withdraw all he wants from one who is infinitely rich. I am, therefore, both a beggar and a rich man."

"Sometimes I compare the troubles which we have to undergo in the course of a year to a great bundle of sticks—far too large to lift. But God does not require us to carry the whole bundle at once. He mercifully unties the bundle and gives us one stick that we are to carry today and then another that we are to carry tomorrow, and so on. We might easily manage it, if we would take only the burden appointed for us each day. But we choose to increase our troubles by carrying yesterday's stick over again today and by adding tomorrow's burden to our load before we are required to bear it."

## The Name of Jesus
### (Song of Solomon 1:3)

How sweet the Name of Jesus sounds
In a believer's ear!
It soothes his sorrows, heals his wounds,
And drives away his fear.

It makes the wounded spirit whole,
And calms the troubled breast;
'Tis manna to the hungry soul,
And to the weary rest.

Dear Name, the Rock on which I build;
My Shield and Hiding-place;
My never-failing Treasury fill'd
With boundless stores of grace.

By Thee my prayers acceptance gain,
Although with sin defiled;
Satan accuses me in vain,
And I am own'd a child.

Jesus! my Shepherd, Husband, Friend,
My Prophet, Priest, and King;
My Lord, my Life, my Way, my End,
Accept the praise I bring.

Weak is the effort of my heart,

And cold my warmest thought
But when I see Thee as Thou art,
I'll praise Thee as I ought.

Till then I would Thy love proclaim
With every fleeting breath;
And may the music of Thy Name
Refresh my soul in death!

John Newton